A Child Shall Lead Them

Stories of Transformed Young Lives at Medjugorje

WAYNE WEIBLE

2004 First printing

ISBN 1-55725-454-0

The messages attributed to the Blessed Virgin Mary given through the visionaries found at the end of each chapter and in the appendix are taken from the official translation supervised and approved by the Franciscan priests at Saint James Church in the parish of Medjugorje.

Library of Congress Cataloging -in- Publication
Weible, Wayne.
A child shall lead them : stories of transformed young lives at Medjugorje / Wayne Weible.
p. cm.
ISBN 1-55725-454-0
1. Mary, Blessed Virgin, Saint—Apparitions and miracles—Bosnia and Hercegovina—Medjugorje—Biography. 2. Medjugorje (Bosnia and Hercegovina)—Church history—20th century. 3. Medjugorje (Bosnia and Hercegovina)—Biography. I. Title.
BT660.M44W42 2005
232.91'7'0949742—dc22 2005016852

10 9 8 7 6 5 4 3 2 1

Published by Paraclete Press
Brewster, Massachusetts
www.paracletepress.com

Printed in the United States of America.

Dedication

I dedicate this book to the memory of Geraldine Loftus. Her struggle in life and courage in death have been my inspiration to write it.

I also dedicate it to the memory of Pope John Paul II, who passed on to his heavenly reward on April 2, 2005—for his personal and public inspiration through his life, his active faith, and his leadership.

And I dedicate it to all of the young people whom I have written about: Their stories give confirmation to the love of the Father for His children.

Contents

Special Message

"Dear children, I am calling you to a complete surrender to God. Pray, little children, that Satan does not sway you like branches in the wind. Be strong in God. I desire that through you the whole world may get to know the God of joy. Neither be anxious nor worried. God will help you and show you the way. I want you to love all men with my love, both the good and the bad. Only that way will love conquer the world. Little children, you are mine. I love you and I want you to surrender to me so I can lead you to God. Pray without ceasing so that Satan cannot take advantage of you. Pray so that you realize that you are mine. I bless you with the blessing of joy. Thank you for having responded to my call."

Message given to the Medjugorje visionary Marija Pavlovic on May 25, 1988.

FOREWORD

The history of humanity often goes the wrong way because it deals with important world leaders, global wars, scientific discoveries, tragedies of all kinds and generally things of the world. It forgets or relegates to a lesser status the simple individual human beings who are the most important participants of history.

These individual human beings who do not pretend to do anything more than live their simple lives in the circle of their family and friends are the principal and leading makers of history. These people make history and history makes them. Unfortunately history often deals with the millions and forgets the individuals.

God is interested in the life of individual people. He wants to make the world a good place for each person. I find this book by Wayne Weible most inspiring because it relates the stories of individual people for whom God came upon the earth and died.

A Child Shall Lead Them does not speak of millions of people who are converting, those we do not know. Instead, it speaks about those people who appear in our lives, those we may know as brother or sister.

To read these pages is to sit with these people and have a comfortable, relaxing time together, maybe drinking coffee, listening and having an enjoyable conversation. When we give the proper attention to people who have names, who are true human beings, not lost in the nameless crowds, we begin the right journey with Jesus who met Matthew and the other disciples and called them to Him.

It is the same with Mary, who met the children in the hills of Bijakovici near Medjugorje and called them to her.

—Svetozar Kraljevic, O.F.M.
Medjugorje, Bosnia-Hercegovina

INTRODUCTION
The heart of a child

It really does take the heart of a child to accept something as awe-inspiring as apparitions of the Blessed Virgin Mary. I discovered that when I went to see and experience this phenomenon for myself in the little mountain village of Medjugorje in Bosnia-Hercegovina. It was there that six children claimed that the mother of Jesus was appearing and speaking to them daily, and had been doing so for nearly five years.

The memory of the final minutes of my first pilgrimage to Medjugorje is as vivid today as it was that crisp May morning in 1986. The transformation to a child's heart reached its zenith for me as our group prepared to board the bus for the journey to Dubrovnik. We would leave the following morning for our homes in the States.

In anguish, I knelt alone behind the church, grasping all that I could out of the last minutes of our stay. I cried as I hadn't cried since childhood, wanting to stay forever in the peace and happiness of that secluded place.

I had arrived in Medjugorje as an adult, convinced the apparitions were truly occurring, but unsure of their ramifications for me, personally. Like millions of others before and after my first visit, I went home transformed into a child of God fully believing and accepting of the graces of this exceptional place.

I now understand why God, through the Blessed Virgin Mary, would choose young people to receive holy messages at

Medjugorje and other apparition sites. The young are in a developmental period before their innocence is slowly tainted and corrupted by the world. They are pure, empty vessels waiting to be filled. The call to conversion, which is the major purpose of apparitions and other supernatural phenomena, is for us to again become like a little one, a repaired vessel in the process of spiritual replenishment regardless of age.

In the rustic, primitive beauty of this simple village nestled in the mountains, the Blessed Virgin began appearing to two boys and four girls. She didn't select the local Franciscan priests or nuns or other persons of importance to be visionaries. Instead, as in past apparitions, she chose children—innocent, open, receptive children.

No one believed little ten-year-old Jakov and teenagers Ivan, Marija, Vicka, Ivanka, and Mirjana—ranging in age from fifteen to eighteen—when they first claimed to have seen a beautiful young lady immersed in a strange light on the side of Podbrdo Hill. The hot, rainy evening of June 24, 1981, would be but the beginning of many such appearances to the children. After several days of apparitions and spectacular miracles, few in the village doubted.

Now, after more than twenty-four years of daily appearances to these children—all of whom are now adults, married, and with children of their own—the fruits of conversion continue to serve as testament to their initial claim. Never in the recorded Marian history of the Church had such an event continued daily for such an extended time. It is as if the Blessed Virgin is standing before the throne of God, saying, "Please, a little more time—it's working!"

It is not surprising that the most dramatic of the conversions occurring through the apparitions at Medjugorje are those of young people, beginning with the visionaries themselves. *A Child*

Shall Lead Them is a collection of such stories, anecdotes, and commentary. This book covers a full range of emotions, trials, and miracles, from heartbreak to happiness. It encompasses young people from toddlers to those in their thirties.

I was personally involved with most of the stories recorded here. Two of them concern my own children. In all of these stories, and in the thousands of others that will never be printed in a book, is solid proof of what happens when a heart is converted to God.

The title for the book is taken from Holy Scripture in the Old Testament book of Isaiah, chapter 11, verse 6: "The wolf shall dwell with the lamb, and the leopard shall lie down with the kid, and the calf and the lion and the fatling together, and a little child shall lead them."

Here is the reason, clearly without debate, why God would choose young people to convey His messages to us. It is at the same time reason and example. Unless one has the spiritual heart and soul of a child, words describing a utopian peace are not easily accepted beyond platitude.

It is *The Child* spoken of in that verse of Scripture, the prophesied and long-awaited Messiah, who gives confirmation in the New Testament Gospel of Luke 18:16-17: But Jesus called them to him, saying, "Let the children come to me, and do not hinder them; for to such belongs the kingdom of God. Truly, I say to you, whoever does not receive the kingdom of God like a child shall not enter it."

What this Scripture verse says to us is that a child is the essence of innocence; conversion is a return to that innocence. That is what this collection of stories is about.

Jesus bluntly tells us in Holy Scripture that we must be "reborn" to enter the kingdom of God. All of us ask: How can we be reborn? For the adult heart, this is a nearly impossible question to answer. However, with the heart of a child, the answer is obvious, as seen in Matthew 11: 25. “At that time Jesus declared, ‘I thank thee, Father, Lord of heaven and earth, that thou hast hidden these things from the wise and understanding and revealed them to babes; . . .’”

May such transformations to a child’s heart continue at Medjugorje and elsewhere until every person possible has an opportunity to allow the child within to lead them to the peace, happiness, and security of being a child of God.

—Wayne Weible

ONE

"Dear children . . ."

In every message given to the visionaries at Medjugorje, the Blessed Virgin Mary begins with these words: *"Dear Children . . ."*

This greeting by the "Gospa of Medjugorje" (*Gospa* is the Croatian expression for "Our Lady") is not addressed to the visionaries alone, but to all who hear, read, or are touched by the messages. All of us are the "Dear children."

Yet, there is special emphasis in the Virgin's messages directed toward the young in age. Never have there been so many snares to distract young people from true belief in God. Alcohol, drugs, and sex top the list, followed closely by family dysfunction. These acute problems of today's youth are a primary motivation for the Catholic Church's intense focus on young people through the late Pope John Paul II's world-wide program of annual youth rallies, which, in all likelihood, will continue under Pope Benedict XVI.

The heart of the Medjugorje message given by the Blessed Virgin Mary is threefold: prayer, fasting, and penance. These are the foundation stones of the Virgin's call to her children in following the path of spiritual conversion. Prayer is the constant she asks for in almost every message. Fasting is to teach and condition us to allow the spirit to rule over the flesh. Penance is the daily call to truly love one another and to help those who are put in our path. In almost every story recorded here these three foundation stones play a key role.

A strong example of the role these elements play in conversion occurred early in my speaking missions. It underlined for me the power of these foundation stones in the conversion of the hardest cases of young people gone wrong.

In October 1985, while watching a videotape about the apparitions of Medjugorje, I felt a strong, personal call by the Blessed Virgin Mary to spread the Medjugorje message. That message is none other than a strong reiteration of the gospel message of Jesus. The mission, if I chose to accept it, would be to speak about the messages and my own conversion through them.

Several years later, I was speaking in a small church located in a suburban community of Pittsburgh, Pennsylvania. It was jammed with people who had come to hear about Medjugorje. By all measures it was a successful evening. People crowded around after the talk, filled with questions. I could see on a majority of the faces a happy sense of awe and wonderment.

Suddenly, a woman pushed through the crowd and grabbed me by the arm. In stark contrast to the others, her facial expression was anxious and stressful. "Please," she said, "you've got to promise me you'll pray for my son. Please ask Our Lady to heal him from drug addiction!"

I assured her I would pray for her son and for her and her entire family, adding that she should pray without ceasing for him as well. "God knows I have," she said tearfully. "I've been praying for him for years and years, but it isn't helping!"

Before I could reply, a young man stepped forward: "Lady, listen to me! You can't give up! I was addicted to drugs and alcohol for more than ten years. My mom prayed and prayed for me and she never gave up. Because of her prayers, I was finally healed, and now here I am in this church listening to a religious talk!"

There was nothing for me to add.

"Dear children, today I invite you to decide for God once again and to choose Him before everything, so that He may work miracles in your life and that day by day your life may become joy with Him. Therefore, little children, pray and do not permit Satan to work in your life through misunderstandings, not understanding and not accepting one another. Pray that you may be able to comprehend the greatness and the beauty of the gift of life. Thank you for having responded to my call."

Monthly message given to the visionary Marija, January 25, 1990.

TWO

Geraldine: A child's courage

People have asked over the years what is the most memorable moment or event in my mission of spreading the Medjugorje message. There have been many, but one in particular comes to mind immediately. It is the story of Geraldine Loftus.

I have never been so touched emotionally as I have been by Geraldine's story, not just from my Medjugorje experience, but in my entire life. Hers is one of two major stories that prompted the writing of this book.

I met Geraldine and her family in Wales, on the first stop of a speaking tour through the United Kingdom in the summer of 1989. She was just ten years old and was suffering from terminal cancer. . . .

Rose Walsch, my hostess, paused after cutting several slices of pie. She had just served us a delicious English meal, and we were about to enjoy dessert and coffee, with plenty of time before my talk that evening. She turned to me and said, "I'm sure this happens everywhere you go, but there is a family here who is in desperate need of special prayers. . . ."

Rose told me about the Loftus family, a devout local family that had suddenly been confronted with the tragic medical diagnosis of terminal cancer in their ten-year-old daughter Geraldine. "To make matters worse," she continued, "they adopted a little two-year-old boy who is mentally handicapped. They purposely adopted him, knowing of his condition, fully prepared to take care of him. And now, this tragic news. Could you please just take the time to pray with the mother, who will be at the talk this evening?"

I never got used to hearing such stories, especially involving children. Assuring Rose that I would definitely pray with the mother, I asked if the little girl would also be at the talk. "Oh, no, she's far too ill," Rose answered, as she set a steaming mug of coffee before me. "Her father is staying home to care for her and the little boy."

I suddenly felt an inner urge that I was to pray over this child. I asked Rose, "Is the Loftus home along the way to the site of the talk?"

Rose stopped in the middle of serving the pie. "It's not on the route, but then, it's not too far away. Why do you ask?"

"Could we stop by on the way? I need to pray over Geraldine and her little brother."

Rose's eyes lit up. "Would you do that?" Before I could answer, she dashed for the telephone and called the Loftus home. Flushed and beaming with happiness, she quickly hung up the receiver. "They would be absolutely thrilled if you came by! I'm sorry, but we'll have to leave right now!" With that, coffee and dessert were left on the table; we piled into the car and headed for the Loftus home.

A grateful father greeted us at the door. "Just last night, we watched a video in which you spoke about Medjugorje, and now you're here!" Terry Loftus was beaming. That was another amazing part of what was happening. The video and the information from Rose and her husband, John, were the first knowledge the Loftus family had of the apparitions at Medjugorje.

Terry led us into his living room. "This is my little Geraldine," he said with fatherly pride. Geraldine got up from where she was sitting on the floor watching television and extended a thin little hand. She was pale and emaciated, and wore a red beanie cap to cover her baldness caused by chemotherapy treatments. She shyly smiled, and her eyes shone with a special brightness. We were immediately friends.

In the twenty minutes we were there, I fell in love with this little girl. Wrapping my arms around her, I asked with all my soul for God to grant a healing, asking primarily that her family would have the peace to accept whatever would happen. As I prayed, I knew Geraldine needed to go to Medjugorje.

At the gentle urging of Rose reminding us of the time, we prepared to leave. I wanted to stay with this child, to spend more time with her. I could only promise her that I would see her again. I knew in my heart that she would be healed. Her healing was initiated with our prayers, but would have to be completed at Medjugorje. I did not know why—only that she had to go.

As we drove in silence, I remembered Our Lady's special message about healing: *"I cannot heal—only God heals."* I also recalled her saying more than once that she needs our prayers and our efforts. To a desperate family, prayer may seem a generic answer by sympathizers. But as is pointed out so often in Our Lady's messages at Medjugorje, prayer serves as the powerful vehicle for the Holy Spirit to do His work.

After the talk, an overwhelmed mother could hardly believe that we had stopped to see her daughter. Through tears of happiness and desperation, Pat Loftus told me of Geraldine's having had two operations for this cruel disease, first diagnosed when she was four years old. "We knew she was seriously ill, but never thought of it as cancer or something fatal."

I promised Pat that somehow, I would arrange for Geraldine and at least one parent to visit Medjugorje as soon as possible.

The following morning, before we left Wales, arrangements were made to get not only Geraldine to Medjugorje, but also her entire family. I was going with a group of kids from our local Catholic school in Myrtle Beach in April, and hoped to get her there at that time.

Of course, the best-laid plans don't always work out. But we come to learn that the Holy Spirit has His way. As it turned out, that was the case with getting Geraldine to Medjugorje at the same time my group was to be there. I would miss connecting with her and her family by a matter of hours. Due to previous speaking commitments, I had to depart for my flight home the morning of their arrival.

Knowing this, I told members of my group who were staying for another day, and other pilgrims, about Geraldine at the talks I gave while there. "I was hoping to pray over Geraldine here in Medjugorje," I told them, "but now I am asking each one of you who see her to pray over her." I emphasized that the Holy Spirit gift of healing is there for all who believe.

Days later when my group returned, I received a telephone call from one man who had taken a special interest in Geraldine. "You can't believe what happened," he said excitedly. "Several of us saw Geraldine shortly after you had left for your flight. She was wearing that little red beanie cap, and her dad was pushing her in a wheelchair. People rushed up to them and began praying over her, telling her that you asked us to do it." He went on to tell me that the visionaries Vicka and Marija had also prayed over her.

I later telephoned Geraldine's father, Terry Loftus, anxious to learn how she was doing. He gave me the news that I was waiting to hear: "We've taken her to her doctors, and the cancer is in total regression!"

It would be the summer of 1991 before I would see Geraldine again. Once again, I was in Wales on a speaking tour. In truth, I had accepted the invitation to return primarily to be able to visit with Geraldine and her family. During the second week of the tour, I arrived at an ancient Franciscan church for Sunday Mass. I was to speak following Mass and was assured by John and Rose Walsch, my hosts for both visits to Wales, that Geraldine and her family would be there.

Entering the overcrowded church, we discovered the only seating room left was in the choir section. I smiled as I began making my way through the crowd, happy that so many had come. As I approached the choir, I heard my name called softly. Turning around, I caught sight of Geraldine and her father standing there. She ran into my arms, and the tears began to flow.

What a joy to see this healthy little girl, now eleven years old, with long, beautiful brown hair and rosy cheeks. I could hardly contain my emotions or take my eyes off of her throughout the Mass.

During the talk, I asked Geraldine to come forward. Having promised her in advance that she wouldn't have to say anything, I told the audience that this is what Medjugorje was really all about. "Here in your midst in the healing of this child is living proof that God loves us, and that if we believe as a child and listen to His messages given us at Medjugorje through the Blessed Virgin Mary, wonderful graces are given!"

I pointed out that Geraldine's healing was a reward for a family that had accepted its crosses, having also adopted a mentally retarded little boy just prior to Geraldine's diagnosis of terminal cancer. They accepted God's will but never stopped asking for a healing of Geraldine or her little brother; he was now also progressing far beyond expectations. This was the living message of Medjugorje, and the result of thousands of prayers from those who knew of Geraldine's illness.

That afternoon, we returned to John and Rose's home, along with Geraldine and her family. I still could not take my eyes off of her and wanted this time to last forever. Like others, I needed confirmations along the way to bolster my conversion journey. This was one of the best.

Rose approached as I sat on her couch talking with Geraldine. "Excuse me, Wayne, I was wondering, would you like that coffee and dessert now?"

I burst out laughing. "Yes, I think it's a bit overdue!"

As Rose served us, I thought of that trip nearly two years ago when we had rushed from her home following dinner for our unplanned visit to pray over Geraldine, leaving coffee and dessert on the table. It was indeed time to have that dessert in happy thanksgiving for the healing of the beautiful young girl sitting next to me.

❧

"Dear children, today also I am calling you to a complete surrender to God. You, dear children, are not conscious of how God loves you with such a great love. Because of it, He permits me to be with you so I can instruct you and help you to find the way of peace. That way,

however, you cannot discover if you do not pray. Therefore, dear children, forsake everything and consecrate your time to God and then God will bestow gifts upon you and bless you. Little children, do not forget that your life is fleeting like the spring flower which today is wondrously beautiful, but tomorrow has vanished. Therefore, pray in such a way that your prayer, your surrender to God may become like a road sign. That way, your witness will not only have value for yourselves, but for all of eternity. Thank you for responding to my call."

Monthly message given to the visionary Marija,
March 25, 1988.

THREE

Geraldine: Part II

Some may ask how it is that a child who is prayed over and seems to be healed, suddenly is struck again with a terminal disease. Some may question whether she was healed at all. I do not; neither does Geraldine's family.

In 1996, the miracle of Geraldine's healing seemed to be nearing an end. I was back in the United Kingdom on another speaking tour and was privileged to spend time with her and her family at their home in Wales. Strong feelings of awe and joy filled me as I marveled at the little girl, now sixteen, who was celebrating life with all the enthusiasm of her teenage years.

But looks were deceiving. Once again, Geraldine was suffering from a bout with cancer. The disease had returned.

The ashen pallor was back along with the loss of hair. One would never know. She wore a beautiful brown wig that fooled me when I first saw her. Her eyes were still full of life, just as they had been when we first met.

Very evident was a bond of love between the child and her parents, a love of hope and confidence. There wasn't a trace of bitterness or pity. That bond was especially strong between daughter and father. Terry Loftus struggled with the condition of his daughter more openly than did his wife, Pat, whose strength was wrapped in her faith.

The Blessed Virgin tells us repeatedly to pray. She tells us to have confidence in God, to approach Him with the heart of a child, to accept *totally* the will of God. Pat was able to do this more openly than Terry. Pat would constantly remind him to accept the will of God but to ask in confidence, to ask for healing, both spiritual and physical.

Outwardly, Geraldine was doing this. She asked me to pray for the young friends she had met in the hospital who were dying of the same deadly disease. She wasn't worried about herself. She knew she had received a special gift as did her parents. They would lean on their faith to carry them through it all.

I would return to see Geraldine in December 1998, this time taking with me my fourteen-year-old daughter, Rebecca. Terry Loftus had telephoned a few days earlier in great distress, as Geraldine had taken a turn for the worse. The purpose of the trip was simply to pray over Geraldine again.

This was an unexpected trip, but one I felt again, by that inner urge, that I was to make. Why Rebecca was supposed to come with me I did not know, but it was part of the same inner urge. We could only hope for a continuation of the miracle of prayer.

Once there, I was glad Rebecca was with me. And so was Geraldine. She was now almost unrecognizable, bloated horribly by the medicines and treatments. Her speech and movements were also altered. Yet, her courage and inner strength were still very much in play, as was the light in her eyes. She and Rebecca hit it off immediately. It was a phenomenal trip, and we returned home with high hopes that Geraldine would recover. Yet, in my heart, I sensed the end was near for my little friend.

❦

Terry Loftus would call from time to time to keep me up to date on Geraldine's condition. It seems she would make progress only to then return to the suffering. Poor Terry was at a loss; there was nothing he could do for her to make her well. After one particularly heavy telephone conversation with him, in which he simply poured out his soul to me, I enclosed myself in my office and cried for a long time.

Two years later, I returned to Wales for what would be my last visit with Geraldine and her family. The disease was still there, but one could not tell it from Geraldine's outward appearance and attitude. The bloating and disfigurement were gone, and she seemed very much at peace; she was enjoying every moment of life as a young woman. "Come on," she said to me as we sat talking in the family living room. "Let's go and have a little treat!"

We went into town, and as we were walking along the sidewalk, Geraldine quietly took my hand and said, "You know, I have a confession to make to you."

What on earth, I wondered, could she have to confess? I waited for her to continue. We walked in silence for a few moments, and then she began to speak: "I was so scared and upset when the cancer returned—and so tired of the constant sickness and pain and suffering! I just wanted to die and be out of this misery!"

"Geraldine, that's understandable under the circumstances—"

She gripped my hand a little harder, interrupting, "No, it was selfish of me. I thought of all of the suffering of my family, all that they had to go through for me. And I thought of you coming here and praying for me constantly and bringing Rebecca with you just for me—and of all the others who have done the same. And then I got mad—mad at myself. I decided if all of you could love me so much and do so much for me, I had to fight harder and to appreciate what was being done for me."

I realized we had stopped walking. Geraldine smiled. "Anyway, that's it; that's my confession. I'm going to continue fighting and appreciating every minute of life!"

My emotions were on edge, and I certainly didn't want to cry in front of this brave young lady. Geraldine suddenly hugged me and exclaimed, "Now let's go have an ice cream!"

The miracle lasted until the early summer of 2001. On June 17, Geraldine Anne Loftus finally succumbed to the disease that had plagued her for more than half her life. While I was expecting the news, it still caught me off guard. I grieved as if I had lost a daughter. A few weeks later, I received a special card of thanks from the Loftus family. In it was a memorial card passed out at her funeral that also contained a special poem of thanks Geraldine had composed two years beforehand, as if in acceptance of her fate. It was a precious gift to all who had helped her, a simple thank you:

Thank you for your generosity
From you to me
Thank you for your kindness
For all to see
Thank you for all your thoughts
It meant the world to me
Thank you for everything
It's a wonderful thing you do
The happiness you brought to me
I hope will come to you!

Geraldine lived a wonderful ten years *more than she would have,* because of belief, confidence, and trust in the power of prayer by her family and friends. In those ten additional years granted through her healing, Geraldine Loftus fully accomplished her mission of life, touching thousands with her courage and peace in the face of such suffering. She will forever be a personal inspiration.

"Dear children! Also today, I call you to prayer. Little children, prayer works miracles. When you are tired and sick and you do not know the meaning of your life, take the rosary and pray; pray until prayer becomes for you a joyful meeting with your Savior. I am with you, little children, and I intercede and pray for you. Thank you for having responded to my call."

Monthly message given to the visionary Marija,
April 25, 2001.

FOUR

Mother to all God's children

From the beginning days Our Lady of Medjugorje made it abundantly clear that her messages from heaven are meant for all of the children of God. They are meant to be heard by every person of every faith. The very fact that I, a Lutheran Protestant, felt personally called to spread the messages underlined the reality of that meaning.

Two incidents occurred in the early days of the apparitions in Medjugorje to lend further proof that Our Lady had come for all of her children. A Catholic priest actually questioned the healing of an Orthodox child accomplished through the intercession of the Gospa of Medjugorje. In response, she told the visionaries, *"Tell that priest, tell all of the people, that those who are not Catholic are no less created in the image of God until they one day rejoin the Father's house. . . ."*

Even more telling was this exchange between the Virgin and her visionaries as she instructed them on holiness. Our Lady actually named a Sarajevo neighbor of Mirjana, a woman named Pasha, telling the visionaries that they should imitate her humbleness and sincerity of faith. "But Gospa," Mirjana exclaimed in wide-eyed wonder, "Pasha is a Muslim!"

"Yes, I know," the Blessed Virgin answered gently, *"you are to convert your own hearts. The rest is for God to decide!"*

In the early days of spreading the Medjugorje messages, I spoke mostly in non-Catholic churches. To my surprise I was asked to speak in the local Catholic Church—that is, the Catholic Church where I regularly attended daily Mass even though I was still a Protestant and a member of a Lutheran church.

Remembering the Scripture about a prophet not being recognized in his own town, I expected little in the way of a response. It was a shock when I arrived that evening to find the church crammed to the hilt.

I was on fire, knowing that many in attendance for the talk were not Catholic. Not worrying about the make-up of the audience, I spoke of the Holy Rosary, telling them of how Our Lady asks us to pray—especially the Rosary—and that with prayer we can stop wars and alter the laws of nature.

Afterward, a young teenager near the back of the crowd came pushing forward, waving a rosary over her head and saying she had to speak to me. When she made her way through, she spoke quietly, her eyes glistening with happy tears. "A lady in the back of the church gave this to me while you were speaking," she began. "Then I heard someone speaking to me, like it was inside of my head. It was a woman's voice, and she was asking me to pray the rosary, but I don't know how to pray it!"

Laughing, I answered. "Wow! That's Our Lady asking you to pray her Rosary. Don't worry. Someone in your family surely remembers how to pray the Rosary and they can teach you."

The young girl shook her head vigorously. "No, no, you don't understand. I'm not Catholic. My family goes to the Southern Baptist Church!"

A powerful illustration of how the Blessed Virgin Mary wishes to reach all of her children with her messages came during a long 1988 speaking tour of the Caribbean island nation of Trinidad, known affectionately as the "Rainbow Nation" because of its large population mix of different races and religions. It had been a hectic tour, with my host Ronald Grosberg setting up more than forty individual talks and interviews. We had spoken at many schools during the day, reaching thousands of young people.

As we drove to the site of the last school talk early in the morning, I thought about one of the highlights of this tour, which had been a large, outdoor ecumenical prayer service in Port-of-Spain, the largest city in Trinidad. The archbishop of Trinidad, as well as leaders of most of the Protestant churches, participated. Thousands came and shared, and for those few precious hours, there were no denominational walls dividing the children of God.

"We're here." The brief statement by Ronald Grosberg, my host for the tour of Trinidad, brought me quickly back to the present as he wheeled his vehicle into a long gravel driveway that led to a large school building. My heart began to pound as I saw a vista of students massed together outside in a tree-shaded area with a makeshift platform near the front of the gathering. That is the way it always was when I was speaking to young people because of the enormous responsibility of affecting their young lives.

"Come on now, do your best. It's the last one," Ronald said with his now-familiar quick pat on the back.

There were several chaotic moments as the school principal tried to quiet the chatter and constant movement of approximately 1,600 young girls. A short introduction brought quiet and I began to speak.

As always, the intimidation quickly vanished as I told of the beautiful events taking place in Medjugorje. I never planned my talks in advance. There were no notes. I simply began, and felt that whatever came was meant for that particular group at that time. It was the Holy Spirit. I was merely an instrument, a microphone for a personalized message to each of the young people, directly from the mother of Jesus.

On this day, I compared the young Medjugorje visionaries to the listening students. I pointed out that at Medjugorje as well as other reported apparition sites the Virgin Mary chose to appear to young people. She chose those young in spirit and age, I told them, to give this all-important message to the people of the world.

For just under an hour they listened raptly. Drawing the talk to a close, I told the girls about Tanya (see chapter 7). I related how this young girl had become hooked on drugs at the tender age of thirteen. She somehow learned of Medjugorje and, feeling drawn to go, begged her mother to take her there in place of having to stay longer in an institution.

There was now a nearly impossible stillness from the 1,600 students as they listened to the story of one of their peers. I continued, telling them that Tanya, like many young people who had come to Medjugorje with a drug problem, had received special attention from the priests. She had met and befriended all of the visionaries and had been allowed to go into the apparition room many times during the actual time of Mary's mystical appearances.

"Yet, this girl was not healed," I related. "Sadly, she became immersed in the drug scene again. Going to Medjugorje, meeting the visionaries, getting into the apparition room—none of these incredible gifts can bring Tanya or you into conversion to God unless *you* accept it." I paused a moment for effect. "Unless *you* say yes to Jesus as Mary said yes to God!"

As the girls remained in a state of unmoving silence, I did something that I had done with young people in Ireland on a tour there two months earlier. It was inspired by what I felt was a special request by the Virgin Mary. I took from my pocket five medals that had been blessed by her at Medjugorje during the time of an apparition, and holding them up I told the girls I was going to pass them out to five students selected at random.

As I moved through the now highly charged crowd of girls, I told them that it was Mary, not me, who decided who was to receive a medal. I began to pass them out to excited and surprised squeals from the recipients, pointing out that receiving a medal did not mean the person was good or bad, and that they were to pray for the entire student body of the school.

After handing the last of the five medals to a girl in the very back of the crowd, I started to make my way back to the platform. After a few steps a girl stopped me and exclaimed excitedly, "You gave that last medal to a girl who is a Pentecostal! She won't know what to do with it!"

"I'm sorry, but Our Lady does the selecting, not me," I answered, smiling, as I kept moving toward the platform. Still, I could not help wondering what would be the reaction of the Pentecostal girl.

As we closed the meeting to thunderous applause, many of the girls immediately surrounded us and began firing questions at us from all directions. It took a good fifteen minutes to make our way to the car.

As I opened the car door, two young girls came running toward us, one of them in tears but smiling broadly. "Oh, thank you, thank you so much for the medal," she exclaimed. "I don't know anything about the Virgin Mary, but I'm going to find out because I believe these messages are real!"

It was the Pentecostal student! Her face radiant with happiness, she continued to thank me over and over. We were finally able to slowly drive through the throng of waving girls and onto the road back to the city.

I looked at Ronald, who was filled with emotion. "How can you possibly be afraid to speak to young people when you have such a thing as that happen?" he said, slowly shaking his head.

"I don't know, Ronald. I simply don't know." I was as happily stunned as he was. In my heart I knew that speaking to young people, no matter how uncomfortable it was, would always be a strong part of my mission.

And I knew that the message was meant for all young people, regardless of their religious denomination.

"Dear children, God wants to make you holy. Therefore, through me He is calling you to complete surrender. Let the Holy Mass be your life. Understand that the church is God's place, the place in which I gather you and want to show you the way of God. Come and pray! Neither look to others nor slander them, but rather let your life be a testimony on the way of holiness. Churches deserve respect and are set apart as holy because God, Who became man, dwells in them day and night. Therefore, little children, believe and pray that the

Father increases your faith, and then ask for whatever you need. I am with you and I rejoice because of your conversion and I am protecting you with my motherly mantle. Thank you for having responded to my call."

Monthly message given to the visionary Marija,
April 25, 1988.

FIVE

Jasmine: A special blessing

An integral part of my Medjugorje mission is to give audiences and individuals a very special blessing from the Mother of God. From the beginning days of my involvement in the apparitions, I have felt an inner urge from the Blessed Virgin to do this. She tells us it is a motherly blessing she obtained from the Holy Spirit, and she asks all who come to Medjugorje to give it to others so that they, in turn, can give it. This blessing is a grace that can heal spirit and body.

The blessing can be given to an individual as many times as desired and can be given directly, or it can be given mentally to someone on the other side of the world. The words are simple and informal: I give you Our Lady's motherly blessing, or, I give you Mary's special blessing, or, I give you Gospa's motherly blessing—however you want to say it.

The most important part of the blessing to remember is that it comes from the Holy Spirit, and thus it is a powerful tool of healing. The story of baby Jasmine is proof of how it can heal when one believes with the heart of a child.

The story of little Jasmine begins with a man named Alfred Lee, a handyman who does small repair jobs mainly in homes. He read a book about Medjugorje and learned of the Blessed Virgin's special motherly blessing. A man with a strong devotion to the Blessed Virgin, Al immediately knew in his heart that the giving of this motherly blessing was to be a singular calling in his own mission of serving God. As he would say later, it struck him like "a bolt of lightning," and he started giving it to all he saw in need.

In October 1996, Al was going through a dark time spiritually. He prayed to the Blessed Mother and to Saint Thérèse, the "Little Flower," as she has become known. He pleaded for a lifting of this darkness, going so far as to ask for a sign of roses that his prayer was heard and the darkness was lifted.

But Al did not receive any roses as a sign of confirmation—at least not in the way he expected. Instead, he began to notice that every child he saw would give him a beautiful smile; these smiles from little children became the roses he sought as a sign. It was for him a total confirmation.

A few weeks later, Al was called to repair a water leak under the kitchen sink in an apartment owned by his daughter. The tenants, Jose and Elizabeth, a young Mexican couple, had two small daughters—Elvira, three and a half years old; and Jasmine, only fourteen months old. Al had previously done small jobs for them but knew them only casually. Elvira appeared to be a bit afraid of him, while little Jasmine was usually sitting in a high chair or lying on the couch or floor. She never seemed to play and was always listless.

After inspecting the sink, Al told Elizabeth he would have to go to a parts store and pick up what was needed to do the repairs. Just before leaving, Al paused at the door and then did something he had never done before. Turning to Elizabeth, he asked her if he could bless her and the children with the special motherly blessing. Normally, he would have done this silently in his heart. The mother was deeply touched and said to him, "Oh, please do give it to us. My little

Jasmine, has a sickness!" Al happily gave the blessing and left, returning with the parts a short time later.

When he returned, Al was greeted at the door by the usually shy Elvira, who was smiling up at him. Another little rose of confirmation, he thought. The young mother was sitting on the couch holding Jasmine. As Al entered the room, little Jasmine jumped from her mother's lap and toddled over to him, holding up her arms. Startled but pleased, he picked her up and kissed her on the cheek. To Al, this was just more of the "roses" he had asked of Saint Thérèse.

All at once, Jasmine's mother Elizabeth looked at him strangely and began to cry. Thinking he had done something to offend her, Al began apologizing, but Elizabeth shook her head, saying, "Oh, no, God bless you! God bless you! You do not understand; these are the very first steps my baby has taken! Jasmine has never walked before, and the doctors said she would never walk!"

Al immediately knew this was a special child's miracle derived from the motherly blessing he had given earlier. Once things had calmed down some, Elizabeth explained Jasmine's situation to him through intermittent tears of joy. Little Jasmine had been totally paralyzed from the waist down since birth with no feeling in her legs due to a form of diabetes. Now, here she was teetering around the room, oblivious to the great miracle of healing that had just taken place through the motherly blessing.

The following day Elizabeth took Jasmine to her doctor, who confirmed that she seemed completely healed, but with a warning that the crippling conditions of the disease could and often did return. A year later, Jasmine was running and playing as a normal child.

Here is a beautiful postscript to this amazing story of a child's miracle healing. In October 1997—just one year later—I was one of several speakers at a conference in Irvine, California. I had learned of Al's story when he sent me a copy of the letter he had sent to the publisher of the book on Medjugorje, telling of Jasmine's healing through the motherly blessing. But I did not realize at this time that he lived in Southern California.

As I was autographing books after my talk at the conference, a man approached, and as I signed his book, he thanked me for telling the story of Jasmine in my monthly newsletter. It was only as he left that something clicked inside of my head. I quickly got up and went after the man, who, when questioned, acknowledged that he was indeed Alfred Lee from the story. "I didn't want to take time away from the others," he said, to explain why he had not identified himself during the book signing.

"Oh, it's no trouble," I answered. "I'm just so glad to meet you. Can you tell me how Jasmine is doing?"

Al smiled and assured me that Jasmine was still healed. He then added, "In fact, she is here at the conference with her entire family!"

I was stunned!

Arrangements were quickly made for me to meet the family later that afternoon. The next day during my talk, I told the story of Jasmine's healing, ending by asking her family to come onto the stage along with Al. Here, I told the audience as I held little Jasmine in my arms, was literal, living proof of God's grace in action through Medjugorje.

"Dear children! Today I invite you in a special way to open yourselves to God the Creator and to become active. I invite you, little children, to see at this time who needs your spiritual or material help. By your example, little children, you will be the extended hands of God, which humanity is seeking. Only in this way will you understand that you are called to witness and to become joyful carriers of God's word and of His love. Thank you for having responded to my call."

Monthly message given to the visionary Marija,
February 25, 1997.

SIX

Out of the mouths of babes

In August 1991, I arrived in Medjugorje leading a pilgrimage that included twelve teenage girls, most of whom were from my hometown. We had an ominous arrival at a nearly deserted airport just outside of Dubrovnik in Croatia. Airplanes had been moved far away, and flights were at a minimum in anticipation of the start of the armed, civil war conflict that would ravage the country for the next three and a half years.

Actual fighting was to begin at any moment. Yugoslav military gunboats lay off the coast, in place and ready for attack. It was just a matter of timing. As for us, our timing couldn't have been worse.

I wondered again, as I had done so often leading up to this trip, why we were coming at this time. Common sense dictated that it was not safe, especially for teenagers. But the people on the trip had insisted on coming—including the teenagers.

Most disconcerting was the parents' conviction that everything would be all right because the young people were going with me, as though I had some special protection since I was spreading Our Lady's Medjugorje messages. That only added to my anxiety. But for some inexplicable reason, I knew we were supposed to be there.

In the setting of Medjugorje it was hard to imagine the threat of war. Flareups had escalated to full battles throughout Croatia. Rumors of troops congregating in these hills for an invasion of Bosnia had me on edge. Worse was talk of clashes in and around Dubrovnik—and at the airport. I prayed that we would be able to leave in a couple of days with no problems. Yet, once we arrived in the village, there was nothing but joy and a sense of safety and inner peace.

As it turned out, it was a wonderful pilgrimage. Everyone, including the teenagers, felt the same love, peace, and happiness that others had felt before the threat of war. The girls had gathered with me each evening for the praying of the Rosary and the apparition of Our Lady. We sat just below the fifth-floor window in the left tower, the place where she appeared each evening.

I had insisted on this evening meeting on the stairs of the church as a compromise with the girls. They wanted to shop, eat pizza, and generally do things teenagers enjoy. They could do all that, I bargained, if they would meet with me on the stairs each evening for the prayers of the Rosary. I further explained the Blessed Virgin's request for prayer. On the first evening, one of the girl's rosaries had turned gold as she prayed the prayers. With that little miracle the rest were immediately on their knees. Suddenly prayer was as important as the other things.

The trip home wasn't easy. Arriving back in the Dubrovnik airport, we found that our scheduled flight had been cancelled. Worse, there were no further flights for that day—or for the rest of the week. After nearly four hours of haggling with airport personnel, we were told that there would be no flight and that we would be put up in a hotel near the Adriatic coast.

Now I was deeply concerned. And scared. That particular location would be right in the line of fire of the expected attack on Dubrovnik.

As I gathered the adults together, trying to figure out just what to do, one of the young girls approached me with a suggestion:

"Mr. Weible, we just came from Medjugorje and Our Lady tells us to pray and she'll take care of us. Why don't we do that?"

Out of the mouth of babes, I thought.

Clearly, this young girl had heard the call. We immediately found a quiet corner and prayed the Rosary. How Mary loves us, I thought! She continues to come to Medjugorje as the Queen of Peace and touch hearts, even into this stench of war. She comes to her children living there even though they are about to engage in a horrible war.

Two hours later, after our travel agent had bargained with the Yugoslav airline officials, an aircraft was sent to transport us to Split and then to Ljubliana, Slovenia, where finally we boarded a Lufthansa jet for Frankfurt, Germany. We stayed overnight there and found enough seats the following morning to return to the States.

I did not relax until I was sure each girl had been reunited with her family. For them, the intense situation in Dubrovnik and the extra day in Germany was exciting drama that only added to an already memory-packed trip.

But the lessons and memories of prayer with these teenagers on the steps of St. James Church each evening, and the powerful Rosary we prayed in the airport, would far outlast the excitement of the last day for all of us. It was a powerful lesson.

"Dear children! Do not forget that you are here on earth on the way to eternity and that your home is in heaven. That is why, little children, be open to God's love and leave egoism and sin. May your joy be only in discovering God in daily prayer. That is why, make good use of this time and pray, pray, pray; and God is near to you in prayer and through prayer. Thank you for having responded to my call."

Monthly message given to the visionary Marija,
August 25, 2000.

SEVEN

Tanya: No longer a child

What happens to innocence when evil mercilessly rips it away from a little soul? Sadly, it results in trauma that forever alters the life of its victim. It happens every day to tens of thousands of children.

This story is about a little girl named Tanya, who lived with her family in Australia. At the tender age of eight, Tanya was sexually abused while under the baby-sitting care of a teenage son of family friends. From the moment of that horror, she could no longer perceive life as a child.

The trauma of Tanya's sexual abuse brought a dramatic change to what had been a very happy life for her and her family. Her parents had immigrated to Australia from their native Croatia shortly after marrying, and were living a good life in the suburbs of Sydney. Tanya and her sister, who was four years younger, were given all the care and attention necessary by loving parents. After the abuse—which occurred numerous times—the peaceful, happy life of a child began to erode for Tanya.

The little girl wanted to tell her mother about the abuse so that she would not take her and her sister to the boy's house anymore, but she was too frightened because he had threatened her. She also feared her mother would not believe her. Desperately, she needed to feel her mother's love and her touch. She began craving attention beyond the norm, using whatever means to gain that attention.

Tanya's behavior became rebellious and destructive, and she befriended others like herself. Two years later, her mother finally learned of what had happened to her little girl when, mercifully, by chance she heard Tanya talking to her sister about it. The relationship with the parents of the boy who had abused Tanya was immediately broken, and shortly thereafter, the family sold everything and moved back to Croatia, settling on an island off the coast. Ironically, they made the move back to Croatia in January 1981, just a few months before the apparitions of the Blessed Virgin Mary at Medjugorje began. This would prove to be a providential move.

But for Tanya, the move to Croatia at that time made matters worse. She was thrust into a new school with new friends in an environment that was totally alien to her. She didn't speak or understand the language very well and was terribly homesick for the country of her birth.

Again, Tanya found friends with mutual problems and a rebellious bent. Soon she was hanging around with them and generally causing hardship for her mother. What she was doing was wrong and she knew it, but it was the one sure way to receive the attention she craved from her mother. She was now smoking and skipping school on a regular basis. Things became worse for Tanya when her father was forced to return to Australia to work because there was no work for him in his native Croatia.

There was a brief interlude in the midst of Tanya's unhappy plunge toward destruction, an opportunity truly provided by God to bring the young girl back to the right path. Her mother, a woman of solid faith, continued to expect her daughters to attend Mass. Tanya, now twelve years old, simply went through the motions and would do whatever was necessary to make the time pass. One Sunday in January 1982, she casually began reading the church bulletin when she noticed a story about the apparitions occurring in Medjugorje. She read it, and while it was at least a distraction from the liturgy of the Mass, she immediately thought it was a hoax, dismissively flipping the bulletin on the pew.

The story about the apparitions, however, would not leave her thoughts. That night as she lay in bed, Tanya prayed to the Blessed Virgin that if the apparitions were really true, let her hear it directly from the visionaries. Straight from their mouths—nothing less would do. She repeated this prayer for several nights.

The troubled teenager was pleasantly surprised a few months later when her mother agreed to let her go with a friend to a convent in Dubrovnik to see her friend's sister receive the habit and become a nun. Surprise turned to shock when she discovered that the Medjugorje visionaries Vicka, Ivan, Jakov, and Ivanka were at the convent as well for a short stay to relieve the stress of daily life as visionaries. It was as if Our Lady were saying to her, "All right, Tanya, here are the visionaries; now ask them yourself if it is true!"

And Tanya did. She asked them outright, and of course, they confirmed to her that they were indeed seeing Our Lady in daily apparitions at Medjugorje. Tanya became especially close to Vicka and spent a lot of time talking to her and taking walks with her.

Unfortunately, the good feelings of peace and happiness from the brief encounter with Vicka and the other visionaries of Medjugorje did not last long. In fact, Tanya went in the opposite direction. Upon returning home, Tanya soon was hanging around again with her friends, who introduced her to a new game—a deadly new game. A group of them would go to a nearby cemetery and hold séances. Soon, her friends were coming to her home and having the séances in her bedroom. It was, according to Tanya in a later interview, the defining moment when evil seemed to completely take over her life.

Tanya started taking pills to calm down after the séances. She began to hallucinate and could not sleep. There were strange voices speaking to her, but there was no one there. At her worst, Tanya felt as though she was seeing the devil himself in the cellar of their home. Pills to calm down advanced to pills to drastically alter her moods. She was soon completely hooked on drugs.

By the age of fifteen, a fully addicted Tanya had overdosed on drugs seven times. Drugs dominated her every waking moment, and to support her growing habit, she began prostituting herself.

Each time before when she had overdosed, Tanya had been confined to hospitals and institutions. She was placed constantly under the care of doctors and psychiatrists by a mother desperate for a cure from the dreaded addiction. This seventh time was different; she had reached the point of no return. Her mother knew—and so did Tanya—that if she re-entered an institution, she could possibly be confined there for the rest of her life.

For her mother, who was left to deal with Tanya's problems since her husband was still working in Australia, there was no choice. Tanya was taken to a psychiatric institution in Zagreb, to remain for an indefinite period of time.

Life in the institution quickly became a nightmare. Tanya was immediately placed on a myriad of medications in an attempt to stabilize her—pills to sleep, pills to wake up, pills to stay happy and out of depression. However, the pills worked the opposite for her. She stayed depressed, very much aware of where she was and the helplessness of her situation.

The young Australian's days were dominated by wandering up and down the halls in pajamas, listening and watching the other patients talking to themselves and fighting with each other. Days of the same monotonous routine turned into weeks and then months, until, after a while, she simply existed.

Finally, after nearly four months of what had become a living hell, there was an interruption in Tanya's bleak existence. Her mother had been summoned to the institution by the doctors to discuss her daughter's prognosis. Upon the meeting between daughter and mother, there was a happy bedlam of tears and hugs. Tanya immediately began begging her mother to get her out of there.

The daughter pleaded with her mother to take her to Medjugorje. She hadn't forgotten about the apparitions or her time with Vicka and the other visionaries. Miracles really were happening there, she believed, and maybe she would be cured of her addiction. After hours of Tanya's arguing, her mother reluctantly agreed to take her to Medjugorje.

Days later, Tanya and her mother were in Medjugorje. They went straight to Vicka's house, where Tanya's mother met privately with the visionary. Vicka recommended they go and see one of the Franciscan priests in the parish, Father Slavko Barbaric, the spiritual guide for the visionaries. He was also a psychologist and had developed a small program there in Medjugorje to help troubled youths. Little did the suffering teenager know that this first meeting with Father Slavko, as well as the events of Medjugorje would, over a long and difficult course, eventually bring her to a healing from her addiction to drugs and alcohol.

I met Tanya in Medjugorje in June 1986, on my second trip there in two short months. I had returned at the invitation of another Franciscan priest, Father Svetozar Kraljevic, to assist him in his writing of a new book about Medjugorje. He, too, had been a spiritual guide for the visionaries and spoke fluent English. Having read his first book and having been deeply touched by its spiritual approach to the apparitions, I was shocked when, upon my meeting him through the leader of our pilgrimage in May, he suddenly asked me if I could return to assist him with the English translation of the new book he was writing. I was back in Medjugorje a month later, excitedly awaiting the opportunity to work with this holy priest.

As matters would have it, Father Svetozar was unable to work with me right away, and I was stuck in Medjugorje with nothing to do for nine days. Worse, there were no other English-speaking pilgrims there at the time. I kept busy studying and editing the manuscript he had given me. Finally, we were to meet the next day at noon.

I arrived at the rectory about forty-five minutes early, settling on a wooden bench below the stairway of the rectory. I pulled out my small travel typewriter and began to go over the notes I had made. Several minutes later, I was startled by the sound of English being spoken to me: "What are you writing?"

I looked up to see a blonde teenager perched on the other end of the bench. "I'm working on the manuscript of a book about Medjugorje, waiting to meet with the priest who is writing it," I responded. Happy to hear an English-speaking voice and noting her accent, I asked, "Are you English?"

"Of course not," she laughed. "I'm from Australia, and I bet you're from America! What's your name?"

With that, introductions were quickly made, followed by non-stop questions and a torrent of personal information. She hardly paused long enough for me to give an answer to a question before popping another one or giving some new and startlingly personal detail of her life. Before long, I knew her entire history concerning drugs and why she was in Medjugorje. She paused only long enough to gauge the shock value of revealing intimate details of her struggles. I learned that she had been in the apparition room at the time of the apparition many times, knew the visionaries quite well, and truly felt that she was being healed.

Our conversation was interrupted as Father Svetozar appeared at the top of the stairs of the rectory, greeting me—and Tanya as well. It was time to go to work. Entering a small side room, as we settled in our chairs I asked Father Svet if he knew Tanya well, noting that he had greeted her by name. Choosing his words carefully, he answered, "Yes, I know Tanya. She has been here for two months now under the care of Father Slavko." Pausing, he continued. "Tanya needs a great amount of help. She has many personal problems. At times, she is very pleasant and nice to be around, but at other times, she is a little—difficult. Just be careful that you do not become too involved."

I assured him that I would keep her at arm's length.

However, keeping Tanya at arm's length was easier said than done. The next morning at Mass, she slipped quietly into the pew beside me, asking if it was okay to sit with me. Later, I learned that it was the first time she had been to Mass in some time. Within a few days, she seemed to find me wherever I might be.

In between editing work on the manuscript, I spent hours talking to and counseling my new young friend. Forgetting Father Svetozar's warning, I felt our time together was helping her. But he would prove to be right; at times she was an angel, and at other times, it was hard to believe the personality transformation in the opposite direction.

One evening after having driven Tanya to her room in my rental car, I was returning later from dropping a friend in Medjugorje, heading for my room in Citluk three miles away. As I rounded a corner, the headlights of the car caught two young girls dancing in the road. I immediately recognized Tanya and was startled that she was not in her room, as Father Slavko had established a rule that she was not to be out beyond ten o'clock at night.

Tanya was just as startled to see me. I brought the car to a halt, demanding to know what she was doing back out of her room. Not wanting to appear weak in front of her friend, Tanya defiantly said she didn't care what Father Slavko's rules were, and that she could do what she wanted. She refused to get into the car at my insistence on driving her back to her room. Frustrated and angry, I drove away.

The following evening was the fifth anniversary of the apparitions, and thousands were at the church grounds in celebration. I hadn't seen Tanya all day and didn't really care, still upset with her from the previous night. I was lost in the serenity, savoring the beauty of the services on the back lawn with friends, when suddenly Tanya appeared, contrite and apologizing for her actions of the night before. "Please come with me," she begged, "I can't pray. I need to talk to you."

As soon as we found a quiet spot, Tanya began to cry. She and her friend had met two boys from the village and stayed out very late. Now she was ashamed and didn't know what to do about Father Slavko. "He'll find out and then he will send me home—what am I going to do? You have to talk to him for me!"

"No," I said firmly. "You're going to tell him yourself, and you're going to tell him the truth."

As she started to protest, I launched into a blunt, tough-love, father-daughter-type lecture. I pointed out to her all the people who had tried to help her and all that had been done for her. Now she had a choice: accept the goodness that was offered to her though her mother's unwavering support, Father Slavko's help, and being in Medjugorje, or go on ruining her life by abusing drugs and by not helping herself.

Again, there was the sudden personality switch. Tanya quietly hugged me and promised to go directly to see Father Slavko after the Mass.

I returned to my friends to celebrate the Mass. Later, Tanya came running up to us, pulled me aside, and excitedly related the events of her meeting with Father Slavko. In a rush of words she said, "Oh, he was furious with me, but said it was good that I had confessed it to him. I told him you told me to do it and guess what—I asked him if he would let you in the apparition tomorrow evening and he said he would!"

I was pleased it had gone so well for her but also stunned at this unexpected gift. Tanya had learned from our conversations that the day after the anniversary was my birthday. This was her special present to say how sorry she was, and was indicative of her angelic behavior for the remainder of my time in Medjugorje.

Several days later, we said our good-byes with a promise to meet again in November when I would return for a third trip to Medjugorje that year. "I'll still be here," Tanya promised. "I love Father Slavko and I want to be completely healed from drugs."

The promise by my young Australian charge would quickly go by the boards. I learned upon my return in November that Tanya had left Medjugorje within days of my departure, running off to Italy with several other drug addicts.

Months later, I heard from Tanya via a telephone call at home. She was back in Australia. Her mother and sister had rejoined her father there and had resettled in Sydney, where her father had found work again. She was struggling to stay off drugs but with fleeting success. "I need to go back to Medjugorje and be under Father Slavko's care," she said. But, she added, she didn't have the money, nor did her parents.

I restated that she had to help herself, that Father Slavko could only do so much for her, and that I would pray for her. But if she didn't do something to help herself, it would all be in vain.

As it turned out, Tanya would indeed return to Medjugorje later for a short stay. To her dismay, this visit didn't change anything. Unfortunately, even being with Father Slavko again, listening to his pleading and scolding, and being in this holy place could not abate her dependence on alcohol and drugs.

Tanya returned home, still on a path to total destruction.

"Today I am happy despite there still being some sadness in my heart for all those who began to take this path and then abandoned it. My presence here is therefore to lead you on a new path, the path of salvation. Thus, I call you day after day to conversion, but if you do not pray, you cannot say you are converting. I pray for you and intercede before God for peace. First, for peace in your heart, then around you, so that God may be your peace. Thank you for your response to my call."

Monthly message given to the visionary Marija,
June 25, 1992.

EIGHT

Tanya: Part II

Not every conversion story coming out of Medjugorje ends on a "they lived happily ever after" note. Such was the case with Tanya. No matter the amount of grace being poured out on a soul, a personal decision to accept the grace must come from the recipient. Tanya, while suffering beyond imagination from her sexual abuse, was given many opportunities. Father Slavko was there to assist her; she was in the apparition room numerous times during the time of the apparition. Many people tried to help her. Still, she was too weak to accept the grace or to help herself.

Yet, as the Blessed Virgin points out constantly through her monthly messages to her children, we must continue to pray, fast, and do acts of penance for lost souls. Only through that continued grace would Tanya find the pathway to healing of body and soul.

Several years later, I returned to Australia for a second speaking tour. When he met me at the arrival gate, my host Leon LeGrand, who also knew Tanya, informed me that she would be at my first speaking site in Sydney. "She wanted to see you right away," he informed me, "but I put her off until the evening of the talk."

I was surprised. Tanya had called my home sporadically, but I had not heard from her in a long time. She had not come to see me on my first speaking tour in Australia. For all intents and purposes, even though I continued to pray for her, she was no longer a part of my life.

Leon informed me that Tanya had become pregnant, had married, and now had a little girl. But it was a troubled marriage, sure to end in divorce. I asked Leon how she was doing with the drug and alcohol addiction. He shook his head slowly. "She won't help herself. Nothing can really be done for her until she decides she wants to be healed and helps herself."

The meeting with Tanya proved Leon right. I was sincerely happy to see her. She assured me she was trying harder, but telephoned me several times during the tour, saying she was going to take drugs again and imploring my help. Worse yet, she was now strongly addicted to heroin.

For what seemed the hundredth time I again told her she had to do something for herself. But this time, although it was difficult, I added: "Look, Tanya, it would be best if you didn't call me or write me until you truly decide you want to be healed enough to follow what Our Lady is asking at Medjugorje. Father Slavko has done all he can to get you to see this." I assured her I would always pray for her and her family. These were harsh words and I felt terrible, but they were necessary.

It was the summer of 2002 before I heard from Tanya again. She had taken me at my word and had not contacted me since my admonition to her in Australia. The premise of her contact now was the death of Father Slavko in late November 2001. After leading a group of pilgrims to the top of Cross Mountain and concluding the journey with prayer, the holy priest who essentially ran most of the programs centered on the apparitions of Medjugorje, suffered a fatal heart attack.

His death was traumatic to all associated with Medjugorje. It was especially difficult for Tanya, who had stayed in touch with him over the years and had come to fervently depend on his spiritual guidance.

I routinely opened my e-mail one morning and was startled to see her name on the list. I opened it and began reading, excited to hear from her. She wrote: "Dear Wayne, you probably don't remember me but I met you in Medjugorje a long time ago. . . ."

She went on to say that she was divorced, was now living with another man, and had another little girl. She missed Medjugorje and Father Slavko terribly and didn't know what she was going to do now that he was gone. As for the drugs and alcohol, she had finally entered a methadone program and had been "clean" for more than three years, even though the urge to use drugs and drink alcohol was still there.

The remainder of the letter spoke at length of how Tanya, now thirty-two years old, wanted to make her life right with God, to truly attempt to live what she had been given through Medjugorje and by the personal guidance of Father Slavko. And while his loss weighed heavily on her, she was determined to embrace the Church again and live in peace with herself.

I was thrilled. Finally, Tanya was taking control of her life.

How could she think I would ever forget her, I began my answer to Tanya. I assured her that I had not stopped praying for her daily since our first encounter. As I wrote, an inner urge struck me: invite Tanya to come to Medjugorje with you on one of your pilgrimages. I immediately added the invitation, telling her that I really felt it was Our Lady asking her to come. Tanya quickly accepted. Soon we were talking via the telephone and making the arrangements for her to join my November 2002 pilgrimage.

❦

Walking along the main street soon after my November arrival in Medjugorje, I came upon Tanya and her oldest daughter, Chantelle. It was a surprising and joyous meeting, as we had previously arranged to meet the morning after my arrival. I learned that Peter, the man she was living with, had insisted on Chantelle's accompanying her mother because, as he said, he was afraid of her going alone. The real reason, I surmised, was to keep her from the temptation of slipping and using drugs again, something she would be reluctant to do with her daughter along.

We talked long into the evening. Tanya kept thanking me, saying that she never thought she would make it to Medjugorje again. I was amazed to see a young woman now before me in place of the little teenager I had first met. There was the pain of a very difficult and traumatic life in her eyes, but also something new—determination. "I really do want to feel good again, the way I used to feel in Medjugorje," she said quietly. "I want to go to confession and receive Jesus again in the Eucharist, because I know that's what Father Slavko would want me to do."

The next day Tanya went to confession. We met later at a small café, and I knew immediately that something was wrong. "He wouldn't give me absolution! Can you believe that? He wouldn't give me absolution!"

Carefully I explained to her the reason why the priest refused to give absolution: her living with another man with no final solution of annulment to her divorce. We again talked for a long time. I told her to try again and to sincerely state her desire to live for Jesus and do what was necessary.

I did not see Tanya for two days after that. When we did meet after the morning Mass, she was once more at peace. "I went to another priest, told him of my desire to be in the Church again, and he gave me absolution!" She paused a moment, looking somewhat sheepish. "I'm afraid I have a confession to make to you. I was so upset and angry after that first priest wouldn't help me that I was going to leave Medjugorje and go home without telling you. But I couldn't do it. I hope you'll forgive me." Not only did I assure her of my forgiveness but commended her for remaining in Medjugorje.

Later, Tanya came to our pilgrimage house and gave witness to our group. She told her story, leaving nothing out. Most important, she stressed the peace of being back in Medjugorje. Tanya told of spending a lot of time at Father Slavko's grave site, praying the rosary there daily. She knew that Father Slavko was with her spiritually. Her trip back to Medjugorje had been a real eyeopener.

"I'm not a perfect human being and I'm not the holiest person you'd ever meet," Tanya told the group. "Some days my prayers are stronger and other days I hardly pray. I no longer use drugs and I have more peace within myself than I ever had in life before. I still struggle with forgiveness and I struggle with letting go of who to blame. I just pray to God that He will give me the strength one day to forgive those people around me who hurt me. To forgive, you have to love, and how do you love someone who hurt you so badly? Father Slavko was right when he told me that the worse sin is not to love, for when you don't love, then hate, jealousy, and anger come creeping into your soul."

These words were a strong indication that Tanya was slowly but surely becoming, once again, a little child of God.

❧

"Dear children, today I want to wrap you all in my mantle and lead you all along the way of conversion. Dear children, I beseech you, surrender to the Lord your entire past, all the evil that has accumulated in your hearts. I want each one of you to be happy. Therefore, dear children, pray, and in prayer you shall realize a new way of joy. Joy will manifest in your hearts and thus you shall be joyful witness of that which I and my Son want from each one of you. I am blessing you. Thank you for having responded to my call."

Monthly message given to the visionary Marija,
February 25, 1987.

NINE

"Adore Him!"

One of the great graces stemming from the apparitions of Our Lady at Medjugorje is the annual Youth Festival. This is a special time reserved for young people to be in Medjugorje, a time specifically set aside to reinforce the love that God has for His little children.

For nearly fifteen years, thousands of young people have made the pilgrimage during the first week of August. Each day, from mid-morning until late evening, young people from around the world participate in singing, praying, attending Holy Mass, and listening to a wide selection of speakers giving personal testimony and inspiration.

The Medjugorje Youth Festival began with a handful of young people coming together in 1989. It now numbers in the thousands, inspired in large part by the Catholic Church World Youth Day rallies initiated by Pope John Paul II.

In organizing the Youth Festival, Father Slavko Barbaric took the Holy Father's inspiration of World Youth Day rallies to the heights it has reached today. The festival has had a domino-like effect. As Father Slavko was inspired by Pope John Paul II, so too, have many followers of Medjugorje been similarly inspired by Father Slavko's call to bring young people to Medjugorje.

One priest in particular took Father Slavko's call to heart. This dear priest friend was an early popular promoter of the Medjugorje message and frequent speaker at Marian conferences. He had a standard answer for fellow priests and others who castigated him for his newfound mission. He would tell audiences:

> I am often asked why I would take youths to Medjugorje since it isn't approved by the Church. My answer is simple: neither is it condemned! In Medjugorje thousands and thousands of teens have become excited about their faith. They go to confession and make night vigils of prayer after climbing a mountain to do it. They spend hours before the Blessed Sacrament. Many of them have become priests and nuns since their experience there. Show me some place in the United States or elsewhere where I can take these same teens, who are bored with Mass and don't want to go to church, teens who don't believe in confession and don't believe most of the teachings of the Church. Show me where I can get the same results, and I will take them there instead!

It was that statement that *inspired me* to want to take *my* children and be a part of it.

❧

I first attended a Youth Festival at Medjugorje in 1996, taking my son Kennedy and two of his friends, Sean and Louis. All three of them were sixteen years old—old enough to understand what was happening there, but young enough to be more interested in the "fruits" of having a good time in a strange new place. Kennedy had been to Medjugorje five times—once with me alone and four times with our family.

Our little pilgrimage arrived after the usual twenty-four hour plane ride and three-hour trek by car from the airport to the village. We would be staying at the visionary Marija's house, even though she and her family would not be there.

Kathleen Martin, an American woman from Miami, Florida, who had actually lived with Marija and her family for several years as a companion and helper, would be taking care of us.

I had known Kathleen for more than ten years. She was totally committed to her faith because of Medjugorje, and Kennedy knew that, having met her before as well. His first question upon learning that Kathleen would be taking care of us was, "Dad, is Kathleen going to make us go to the church and pray all day?" This was his one reservation about making the pilgrimage, and of course, he had convinced the others that "going to church and praying all day" was a real possibility.

I laughed. "No, of course not, but I do expect you to go to Mass each day and to participate in the daily programs, which include the evening Rosary and the apparition."

"We've got to go to the church *two* times every day?"

"Yep—other than that, you can go and do what you want."

After a few more groans and grudging acceptance, the matter seemed to have been settled.

Yet, the next morning after I roused the boys from bed to prepare for the regularly scheduled mid-morning English-language Mass, their objections started: They were too tired from the long journey there; it was too hot and too long a distance to the church to walk through the fields; why didn't we at least have a car to drive to the church? This became their mantra for the next two mornings prior to the start of the festival. In between, they were having a ball.

That Wednesday, the festival was scheduled to begin with a late-night hour of Eucharistic adoration. After the morning Mass, the boys disappeared and did not return to the house until mid-afternoon. They came in red-faced and drooping with exhaustion. "Where have you guys been?" I asked.

Kennedy could barely speak. "We decided to climb that mountain, and we nearly died of heat stroke because we forgot to take water!" After downing multiple glasses of cold drinks and a light lunch, they flopped in their beds, not to be roused before the evening trek to the church for the Rosary and the time of the apparition. I didn't have the heart at that time to tell them that we would be making a third trip to the church that night.

As we finished a late dinner, I took a deep breath. "Uh, guys, don't wander off, because we're going back to the church in about an hour or so for the start of the festival. . . ."

Eyes widened and mouths were agape. "Dad, you've got to be kidding us—we're wiped out from climbing the mountain. Please tell us you're joking!"

"Sorry, but I'm not joking. This is what we came here for." I paused a few seconds as the inevitable registered with them. Hoping to ease their anguish, I added, "I do have some good news. Kathleen borrowed a car, and we're driving tonight instead of walking through the fields."

Arriving at the adoration site, which would be at the outdoor altar at the rear of St. James Church, the boys were surprised to hear joyful music being played over the PA system, and to see thousands of young people filling all of the benches in the field in front of the altar. "That's okay," I said, "you can kneel here on the steps of the altar." We settled on the lower cement steps on the left side of the altar, the boys resignedly dropping to their knees and lowering their heads. I wasn't sure if they were preparing for prayer or sleep!

The adoration service began as the music switched to soft background accompaniment. The crescendo of verbal noise changed to meditative silence. Nowhere in the world is there adoration like there is in Medjugorje. It was a personal, intimate hour of ongoing prayers in a multitude of languages interspersed with spiritual songs. The boys never moved from their initial kneeling with heads bowed. Again, I wondered, were they paying attention? Was this powerful hour of holiness reaching their young hearts? Or, were they asleep!

I soon received my answer. The service was over and the cacophony of chattering noise returned. The boys were on their feet now, but immediately I noticed they were very quiet. Louis turned to me, and I could see that haunting look in his eyes that I had seen before in so many people coming to Medjugorje. He had been touched. In fact, it appeared that all three of them had been touched.

"Mr. Weible," Louis said, slowly shaking his head, "why don't we do this in our church back home?"

"I don't know, Louis, I really don't know, but we can check into it when we return."

In that fleeting moment, I knew exactly what my priest friend had meant in his answer to critics who questioned his taking young people to Medjugorje. And I knew that I would make it a part of my mission to do the same.

"Dear children, today I invite you to fall in love with the most Holy Sacrament of the altar. Adore Him, little children, in your parishes! And in this way you will be united with the entire world. Jesus will become your friend and you will not talk of Him like someone whom you barely know. Unity with Him will be a joy for you and you will become witnesses to the love of Jesus that He has for every creature. When you adore Jesus, you are also close to me. Thank you for your response to my call."

Monthly message given to the visionary Marija,
September 25, 1995.

TEN

Goran: From raging hatred

As I concluded my final interview with Goran Cukevic, he was suddenly filled with emotion. Struggling with limited English, he said, "I cannot tell you how much hatred was inside my heart for such a long time. I hated everything and everyone."

It had become clear from listening to Goran's story that feelings of hatred had begun festering in him at an early age. Tragedy seemed to take up residence in the Cukevic household, located in Split, Croatia. It began when his four-year-old younger sister fell out of the fourth-floor window of their apartment and was killed; his younger brother contacted meningitis when he was just a year old and was left deaf and unable to speak; and his father was away from the family home for long periods of time working as a seaman to support his family as best he could. To top it off, Goran's mother was diagnosed with leukemia.

As each succeeding tragedy weighed the family down, six-year-old Goran Cukevic was left to cope on his own. He found solace in friends who were usually older than he and were doing wrong things. He remembers his first conscious act of doing wrong: He took a bar of chocolate from a small nearby store and then lied about it.

Within the next two years, Goran was routinely committing such acts. He constantly took money from his mother's purse. She hardly noticed or cared, because by this time, she had fallen into a long siege of depression. There was no time for her little son.

By age eleven, Goran—now known to all of his accomplices by the nickname "Cuke" (pronounced CHEWKEH)—was introduced to alcohol by his older companions. The nickname seemingly represented the beginning of his emerging alcohol and drug-infested life. Emboldened by drink, Cuke started committing acts that normally he would be afraid of trying, including stealing cars. By thirteen, he was a hardened delinquent, bordering on a full life of crime.

And then tragedy struck its severest blow: Cuke's mother died. Despite his tough ways, he took her death extremely hard. He wanted to die, too, and he told everyone that he was going to kill himself. No one took him seriously, thinking that he was expressing his grief over his mother's death, and that his threats would pass. On the first anniversary of her death, young Cuke attempted suicide. He took a pistol and shot himself in the head. The bullet lodged in his brain in a way that would make the bullet too dangerous to remove. It remains there to this day.

From that first suicide attempt, life plunged rapidly downhill for Cuke. Depression pushed him into more alcohol abuse, eventually leading to marijuana and later to hard drugs. Heroin soon became the new addiction of choice, and, as Cuke would say later, it "opened the doors of hell" for him.

It took a couple of years for Cuke's father to discover just how far into the world of darkness his son had sunk. He tried reasoning with his son, and when that didn't work, he beat him and screamed at him. Finally, exhausted and at his wits end, he resorted to psychiatry. He placed Cuke in the psychiatric unit of Split Hospital. This was another lost opportunity for healing, because his son's "friends" would come to visit him and bring him drugs.

During these worst of times, a tiny flicker of hope and a chance for some semblance of normalcy—a chance to be "Goran" again—came into Cuke's life. He met a girl named Zeljka, and they became close. But eventually, because of the drugs, he began to abuse her. If it came to a decision to use drugs or be with Zeljka, he chose the drugs.

Zeljka truly loved Cuke, but like his father and others, she finally caved in and began taking heroin with him. Later, Zeljka became pregnant. This was a predicament but also an opportunity for them both. In her third month, she pushed Cuke to change the way of life they were leading and to begin a new life as a family. But Cuke wanted nothing to do with responsibility, having sunk far too deeply into the drug life to care about anyone but himself. He decided she should have an abortion. Sadly, Zeljka gathered the necessary money needed for the abortion and gave it to Cuke so that he could pay the doctor. Cuke sent Zeljka to the doctor's office and then took off with the money to buy more drugs.

Inevitably, Cuke ended up in jail. His father decided that it was better for him to remain there and did not work for his release, thinking that this horrible experience might knock some sense into his son's head. But it didn't; Cuke was now a hardened criminal. Upon Cuke's release his father arranged for him to get a job working in the warehouse of the company where he was now employed. Once again, Cuke took advantage of the good offered to him and turned it into an easy way to find money for his drugs. He stole everything he could from the warehouse and sold it.

This was too much for his father. The family was disintegrating in the wake of Cuke's life of darkness. After his release from yet another stay in jail, Cuke's father confronted him. Cuke recalled with obvious pain the blunt words of his father:

"You have a right to destroy yourself, and I can't stop you. But you don't have the right to destroy the rest of us. You go out there and you take as many drugs as you want to, drink yourself to death if you want to, but don't come back here while you're doing it. Only if you decide to be a man can you come back to this home, and then I'll help you."

At that moment Cuke hated his father, hated the whole world, and blamed the whole world for his terrible life. The little Goran that lived before tragedy, alcohol, and drugs, was, for all intents and purposes, dead.

During this entire period of darkness, Cuke never thought of turning to God for help. His family was Catholic, but to him their faith was just a tradition. He had attended catechism lessons and even served as an altar boy, but only because he was made to do it. Thus, there was no cry for help to God. His misery would become even worse before poor Cuke would reach out through faint remembrance of the Blessed Virgin Mary.

That misery would include spending over two years in a criminal asylum. Cuke escaped, was captured, and returned to the asylum where the head doctor took him into a room and beat him almost senseless, telling him, "I am god here. I can do what I want. I can kill you if I want."

By the time he was to be released from the asylum, most of Cuke's teeth and hair had fallen out. He hadn't taken a bath or shower for years. He was so frightened of the outside world that the night before his release, he once again tried to take his life: He took a razor and cut his veins. The doctors at the asylum simply patched him up and threw Cuke out the next morning.

Back in Split, even though the toll on his body had been pushed to its limits, Cuke started taking drugs again as soon as he was able to obtain money through criminal acts. Sleep came in small increments. Now too weak even to break into houses, Cuke was shunned by other druggies and drug dealers.

Finally, on a freezing cold night in the early winter of 1996, Cuke hit rock bottom. He crawled through the broken window of a derelict house and lay down on a piece of cardboard, dropping into a fitful sleep until nightmares awakened him. There was nothing left. He had tried to kill himself so many times, but always at the last minute, someone would patch him up enough for his torturous existence to go on. He was now thirty years old and had nothing: no family, no girlfriend, no friends to help him. Rock bottom was the full realization of what he was and where he was.

With nothing left, Cuke cried out for help to the Mother of God. He tried to pray, using the only words he could remember: "Hail Mary, holy Mary, pray for us!" It was all coming out wrong, but he didn't care. "Please, Our Lady," he cried through body-wracking sobs, "either take me to you so that I finish this miserable life, or else show me the road to get out of all this!" For several more days and nights he cried and prayed.

Early in the morning of the fourth day, Cuke managed to drag himself to a small park near the deserted house. As he watched people come and go, all he could think was, "What will I do. . . ?"

Cuke watched as a woman approached him. What did she want? Had he robbed her at some point in time? The woman said, "Good morning," and then said she had a problem that possibly Cuke could help her with. Cuke interrupted her in a weakened, raspy voice saying, "Listen, lady, I have more problems than you can even think of, so just leave me alone."

The woman was undeterred. "I am looking for a young man who goes by the nickname of Cuke," she went on. "I was told he hangs around here, and I'm wondering if you could help me find him."

Cuke was shocked. Had he heard her right? Should he identify himself or would that cause more trouble for him? And then he thought, what more could possibly happen to me? and said, "That's me, I'm Cuke." The lady started to cry.

The woman explained that she was the mother of another lost son addicted to drugs and living on the streets who had landed in jail. When she identified her son, Cuke realized he wasn't a close friend—just someone he had known on the streets who had ended up in jail. The mother said that every time she went to the jail to visit her son, he would tell her somebody has to help this guy Cuke. "He's going to kill himself. Somebody has to find him and help him." The woman finally managed to get her son out of jail and into the Cenacolo Community, the drug rehabilitation center at Medjugorje. She then came looking for Cuke.

Cuke wouldn't realize it for some time, but his prayers were being answered. How appropriate that the Mother of God would send the mother of another lost son to rescue one of *her* lost sons.

It took several days for Cuke to respond. The drug habit was still at work. But when he ran out of drugs, he would go looking for the woman, who was busy arranging papers and identification for him. Despite how dirty he was, she took him into her home. One day she came to him with a bus ticket. She took him to the bus station and told the driver Cuke was not to get off until the bus reached Medjugorje. She told Cuke that

Our Lady was appearing there. But, she added, Cuke must throw away all of his drug paraphernalia before boarding the bus. For unexplained reasons, Cuke went along. He still did not associate this turn of events as Our Lady's intercession in answering his plea made in desperation.

On arriving in Medjugorje, Cuke went to Cenacolo. They had food there and beds. In his mind, this would do until winter was over. He was immediately taken in, and the beginning of a new life started.

Cuke soon discovered that life at Cenacolo was harder than all the years he had spent on the streets. For the first time in a long time, he had to actually look at himself in a mirror and see what he had become. He had to come to grips with the fact that he had created the dark life. He didn't know how to speak without cursing, and he had to fight against the pull for drugs. But he had help—other recovering drug addicts, including the son of the mother who had rescued him. There was only hard work and prayer as treatment, and the company of others with life stories frighteningly similar to his. But one advantage many of them had over him made him sad and jealous: They had families to help and support them.

One day Cuke was asked to show a group from Split around the facilities, since he was originally from that city. He came into the room to greet the group and was shocked to see his father among them. He could hardly look at him, so filled was he with shame and guilt at what he had done to his family. But his father reached out his hand to him and started to cry. Soon they were embracing and kissing amongst tears of utter joy at seeing each other. Before his father left that evening, Cuke promised him that he was going to stay in the community and try to recapture and replace a life of darkness with one of light.

❦

It was the beginning of the return of "Goran" Cukevic to the real world of goodness and righteousness. He would continue to be called by his nickname, Cuke, but Goran, the little son, was returning as Goran, the man. Three years and eight months later, Goran left the community and reentered the world. He had made peace with himself, with the world, and with God through the loving intercession of Gospa.

Goran worked for the Franciscans at Medjugorje, doing whatever needed to be done, including a long tour of cleaning the public toilets next to the church. Eventually, the friars gave him the responsibility of handling the collection money from each Mass. Goran would later say that the trust the Franciscans placed in him by giving him this task did more than anything to complete his healing.

In spite of the huge transition from his previous life of darkness to one of light, there was one huge thing missing from Goran's life—someone to intimately share it with. Thank God he had his family back, but how he longed for what he had lost with Zeljka—a chance to begin his own family. Goran felt that no one would want a former criminal and drug addict. Who would possibly want their daughter to marry someone like him? He prayed that Our Lady would intercede and help find someone for him.

And, the Blessed Mother did. A young lady named Katarina from the Czech Republic came to live for a while in the village of Medjugorje. She had been deeply affected by the apparitions and wanted to spend more time there helping where she could. Goran fell in love with her at first sight.

Katarina was beautiful, deeply devout in her faith, and without any of the horrors in her life that Goran had suffered through. She was thirteen years younger than he. He fell more and more in love with her, but from afar, never daring to think that she could care from him. Incredible as it was for Goran to believe, Katarina also fell in love with him.

Goran and Katarina were soon married, and with the help of Goran's father, they began building a small home on the outskirts of the village. A year later, they were blessed with the birth of their daughter, Lucia. Goran works at making icons and sells them when he can. There is little income for his family, but he continues working where he can.

For a while, Goran was given the job of organizing and running a small, government-run drug center a short distance from Mostar. It is a miniature copy of Cenacolo, with ten to fifteen residents at any given time. The late Father Slavko Barbaric had recommended Goran for the job to the center's director. When asked if he could trust this man who had been so addicted to drugs, Father Slavko had replied: "Trust him? I would entrust the whole of Mostar to him!" This was a recommendation that remains very dear to Goran.

Goran is now happy and secure in the love of God. He put it succinctly as we ended the interview: "The solution, you see, is not just to stop taking drugs. It can only come from changing yourself, by turning to God and putting Him in the first place in your life."

In July 2004, while in Medjugorje for the Youth Festival, I attended a celebration at Goran and Katarina's home in honor of the baptism of their two-week-old son, Juka. In attendance were Goran's father and brother, as well as the son whose mother had been sent to rescue Goran from the streets. Her son, Djani, is now one of Goran's closest friends. They had spent years together in Cenacolo. He, too, is married and the father of two children, with his wife expecting in the fall. Both couples are part of a prayer group that meets weekly at one of the homes of the participants.

Life is not easy, and there are heavy obligations with Cuke's growing family. But for Goran "Cuke" Cukevic, the hatred that dominated his soul has been totally eradicated by the light of God's love.

❧

"Dear children! I want you to surrender your hearts to me so that I may take you on the way which leads to the light and to eternal life. I do not want your hearts to wander in today's darkness. I will help you. I will be with you on this way of discovery of the love and the mercy of God. As a mother, I ask you to permit me to do this. Thank you for having responded to my call."

Annual message given to the visionary Mirjana,
March 18, 1999.

ELEVEN

"Let Satan know you belong to me!"

The stories of Tanya and Goran underscore the truth that spiritual conversion is an ongoing struggle for the souls of humanity. It is God against Satan; light over darkness; peace versus war.

The Blessed Virgin Mary came to Medjugorje as the Queen of Peace. Even before her arrival on the evening of June 24, 1981, the Prince of Darkness was already there to do everything possible to take away the peace she would bring to the people. The new battlefield for souls, and arguably, one of the most important of modern times, would be the village of Medjugorje and its extension through the apparitions. I firmly believe this.

On August 2, 1981, the same day the miracle of the sun was first witnessed in Medjugorje, a strange event took place later in the evening. It was a frightening and bizarre event that would leave no doubt in the hearts of the participants that not only was the Mother of God present in their village, but so was her declared adversary, Satan.

The day was one of celebration. It was the Feast of Our Lady of the Angels. Excitement among those in attendance was at a fever pitch, because many of them had witnessed the miracle of the sun. No one wanted to go home. A small group of teens, who had formed into a dedicated prayer group overseen by the visionary Marija, asked her and the other visionaries to join them in the fields so that they could go on with their prayers and singing. The visionaries readily agreed to join them.

After the Mass, the group gathered with the visionaries in an isolated field away from the church. Word had spread about the impromptu gathering, and many adults also were there. After several songs and prayers, the Blessed Virgin suddenly appeared to the visionaries. Marija startled the gathering when, after a few minutes in ecstatic conversation with the Virgin, she turned to the group, smiling broadly, and said, "Our Lady says she will allow those who so desire to come and touch her."

The people rushed forward to "touch" the Virgin. The visionaries would tell them: "You are touching her veil . . . now you are touching her dress!" Suddenly Marija shouted: "Oh! Our Lady is disappearing and she is completely blackened!"

Marija then announced solemnly, "Our Lady says there are many here who have sin on their souls and that we should all go to confession tomorrow!" The following day, all of the Franciscan priests were busy hearing confessions in and around the church. This went on for hours.

That day would mark the beginning of a daily evening routine at St. James Church with praying of the Rosary, ongoing confessions, and Holy Mass. It would also serve an ominous notice that Satan would do all he could to counter the graces being poured out in Medjugorje. Marija later revealed that just before coming to the field, she had stopped at her home to change into jeans. The Virgin immediately appeared to her and somberly warned that Satan was indeed there to take away the peace that she was bringing to them.

The struggle for souls has raged on. Our Lady has asked, pleaded, urged, and implored the world through a constant stream of messages to adhere to her formula for defense against the attacks of Satan: pray, fast, and do penance. Nearly three years later, the Blessed Virgin would say to the people through a message to Marija, *Take your rosary in your hands and let Satan know that you belong to me!*

The disquieting events of that day at Medjugorje in August 1981 would be recalled in chilling fashion years later as I finished speaking to a group of middle-school students at a large Catholic church in Atlanta, Georgia. The audience of fifth- to eighth-graders had listened intently as I told them about Our Lady and her messages. So had an unexpectedly large contingent of adults who had joined the students.

During the talk, I had related to my mixed audience the events of that August day in Medjugorje when the Blessed Virgin Mary had warned the visionary Marija that Satan was there to take away the grace she was giving them through her apparitions. I went on to speak of how they, the students, were now old enough to understand the difference between good and evil. "He will do everything possible to keep you from believing in God and living by His commandments. You have to be on guard." I held up my rosary. "This is a good way to protect yourself," I continued. "Our Lady even said in a message that we should take the rosary in our hands to let Satan know that we belong to her."

Now, as I finished the talk, I remembered there was one more thing to do.

A lady had brought a large plastic bag of wooden rosaries she had purchased in Medjugorje. "I just thought you all could give them to the children since they come from

Medjugorje and have been blessed during an apparition," she said, as she handed the bag to Mary Elkins, who with her good friend JoAnn Haymon had arranged my speaking itinerary in the area.

Mary turned to me. "How do you want to do this?" she inquired.

Ever the skeptic, even after all the years of seeing how heaven works, I didn't think we could give away that many rosaries to kids of this age. "Well, we'll give out what we can. Maybe some of the adults will want one. I'll tell the kids after the talk that you guys will have them, and if they want one, to see you up front here over near the statue of Our Lady."

I motioned toward the statue in the forward right corner of the church. Prior to the talk, one of the parishioners had made it a point to show me the statue. It was a large, beautiful, solid wood carving of Our Lady, sitting firmly on a heavy marble stand. According to the parishioner, it was very old and had been in several churches in the diocese before finding a home in this rather new sanctuary.

"I want to do one more thing before we close," I told the audience. "A lady brought one hundred rosaries from Medjugorje, and she gave them to us so that we could give them to any of you young people who might want one." I pointed to Mary and JoAnn, who were standing about ten feet in front of the statue. "Those ladies will pass them out on a first–come, first-served basis after the talk."

Hardly had I finished making the sign of the cross after an ending prayer, when there was a near stampede toward Mary and JoAnn. Young hands reached out imploringly for a rosary. Within a few seconds all but one rosary was given away. JoAnn had the last rosary and there was still a sea of hands wanting it. "What should I do?" she asked in near panic.

"Just give it to one of them," I said, laughing, amazed at the response.

As JoAnn handed the last rosary to a girl, there was a loud crash, and everyone froze. The statue of the Blessed Virgin Mary had toppled over onto the floor!

"Who did that?" one of the teachers yelled.

There was an elderly couple sitting near the base of the statue. The woman looked at the teacher, shaking her head. "The children didn't do that—it just fell. It fell all by itself. We were sitting right here and saw it happen!"

The stunned silence was broken when a girl student standing near me said, "Oh, wow, Our Lady must be really upset with us for fighting over the rosaries."

"No," I said, "that isn't how Our Lady does things. That comes from the evil one."

There was no need for further explanation.

"Dear children, today, like never before, I invite you to prayer. Your prayer should be a prayer for peace. Satan is strong and wishes not only to destroy human life, but also nature and the planet on which we live. Therefore, dear children, pray that you can protect yourselves, through prayer, with the blessing of God's peace. God sends me to you so that I can help you if you wish to accept the rosary. Even the rosary alone can work miracles in the world and in your lives. I bless you and I stay among you as long as it is God's will. Thank you for not betraying my presence here, and I thank you because your response is serving God and peace. Thank you for having responded to my call."

Monthly message given to the visionary Marija,
January 25, 1991.

TWELVE

Marie: Saved by a mother's love

Is there anything more powerful than a mother's love? Most of us would answer no, based on our personal family experience. While the father is the head of the household, the mother, with her constant nurturing, is the force that keeps it together.

As a child, Veronica knew there was something different about her family. They seemed more attentive in the practice of their faith than most of the other families in her Korean community. A majority of the credit for the family's faith was due to Veronica's mother, and she heavily influenced the same trait in her daughter. However, both parents had a strong devotion to the Blessed Virgin Mary, a devotion passed on to the children by daily teaching and example.

It was not surprising to her parents when Veronica married a man of strong faith. With the birth of their first child, she decided with her husband's blessing to consecrate their newborn little girl to the Blessed Virgin Mary. Her little girl, whom she named Marie (not her real name) grew up beautiful and smart, with a sweet and humble personality. She was truly their pride and joy.

Marie was an excellent student from first grade on. Later, she was accepted into a top, private, Catholic high school. She was a happy child who was always obedient. Mother and father were proud. Their little girl was developing just as they had hoped and prayed she would. Then things began to change.

During Marie's freshman year at the school, she began to cause a bit of trouble. In the beginning, it was nothing too serious—just the usual adolescent misbehavior. She still maintained good grades and was enrolled in a few honors classes. But as Marie entered her sophomore year in high school, her change in personality led her from small trouble to sticky situations of bad behavior and insolence toward her parents.

The caring, loving mother was confused. What had she done wrong? She had closely followed her own mother's teaching. Veronica rationalized that Marie's change in personality was just a bad case of raging teenage hormones, and even though her daughter was out of hand at times, she tried to accept her as she was. Rationalization was replaced by shock and denial when word reached Veronica from other parents that her daughter might be "tinkering with drugs. . . ."

The thought of her daughter's using drugs had never crossed Veronica's mind. Was this the reason for the change in Marie from model child to prodigal daughter? That was something that happened to other teens or young people in movies and TV shows. Not her daughter. Not sweet little Marie, dedicated to the Blessed Virgin Mary.

As time passed, Marie's life, as well as her mother's, went from difficult to a living hell. Her roller-coaster mood swung from one end of the spectrum to the other. She seemed to be angry at something or someone all the time. Worried about her condition, Veronica had to drag Marie to psychologists for medical diagnosis and treatment. After several attempts to determine the problems and a course of treatment, Marie refused to go to any more appointments. "It's a total waste of time and money," she screamed at her mother. "None of this is helping!"

It was at this critical juncture that Veronica discovered Medjugorje. A church friend, commiserating with her over her predicament, lent her the book *Medjugorje: The Message.* Discouraged at the total collapse of her relationship with her daughter, the mother had all but given up hope it could ever be restored. She took the book and promised her friend she would read it—doing so only to get her off the subject. Nothing had worked to this point; there was no reason to think some book was going to change anything.

A flicker of hope kindled as Veronica began to read the book. It related how the Virgin Mary was appearing every day to children who were her daughter's age. People were being healed there from disease and addictions. That caught her eye. The more she read, the more convinced she became that she was being called to go there. Childhood memories of prayers to the Blessed Virgin Mary with her parents flooded Veronica's thoughts again. If she went to Medjugorje, she thought, she would surely find some kind of answer to help her daughter.

To her amazement, Veronica discovered that a group from her church, and other churches in the area, was going to Medjugorje on pilgrimage. It was December 1997; the civil war that had raged in former Yugoslavia, though still smoldering, was finally over. It was again safe to go on pilgrimage to Medjugorje.

Buoyed by this chain of events, Veronica decided to take Marie with her. By now, Marie was completely out of touch with her faith. The only reason she went to church on Sunday was because her parents insisted. But Veronica's hope was once again shattered as Marie angrily responded to her mother's offer to take her to Medjugorje: "Why would I want to go to such a poor country that's still under war, and for what?"

Well, Veronica thought, even if her daughter wouldn't come with her, she would still go and pray for her. She was convinced by some inner intuition that the answer to Marie's problem was there.

Veronica arrived in Medjugorje with her son John and her mother. She had convinced them to come with her, thinking that the more family members there were to pray for Marie at Medjugorje, the better. They arrived in time to attend Christmas Eve Mass at St. James Church in Medjugorje.

On Christmas day in the cold and snow, Veronica climbed Cross Mountain alone. She climbed with bare feet as a special penance, praying for her troubled daughter. Yet, once back in her room, nursing the small cuts and bruises to her nearly frozen feet, she didn't feel anything had changed. She had poured out her heart in prayer to the Blessed Mother and had taken these drastic steps of climbing barefoot in the cold. Still, there were no direct answers to her troubles.

Veronica had come to Medjugorje hoping to actually see the Virgin Mary through a vision. But there was nothing—no visions, no words of comfort or guidance spoken to her aching heart. It was so unfair, she thought; others in her group seemed to be deeply touched by Medjugorje. Some were claiming to have had personal visions, witnessing the miraculous sign of the sun spinning and other things. Everyone seemed to be having mystical experiences except Veronica. And it wasn't because she didn't try. She spent hours in the chapel, gazing at the statue of the Virgin Mary and weeping. "Please, please, dear Mother Mary," she cried, "help my daughter!"

In the fall of 1998, I was speaking at a church in Los Angeles, California, close to where Veronica and her family lived. As I answered questions and signed books afterward, I noticed a well-dressed Korean woman nervously standing a short distance away. Her actions indicated that she wanted to approach, but she kept hesitating. Finally, when almost everyone had left the area, she timidly came forward. "I want to ask a big favor of you. You seem so close to the Blessed Virgin Mary, can you please pray for my daughter? She is so lost in faith, and I just don't know what to do. . . ."

Veronica proceeded to give me a short history of her daughter's change in personality, and she told me how she was only now accepting the bitter truth that Marie was addicted to drugs. She related how her beautiful little girl, whom she had consecrated to the Blessed Virgin Mary, and who had been such a sweet, innocent child, was now emaciated and unhealthy, with dark bags under her eyes. "I finally got the courage to confront her and ask her—because I'm her mother and I knew something wasn't right— what was the matter with her." Veronica dabbed at her eyes. "But she stubbornly resisted and claimed that nothing was wrong with her. She has no motivation and she doesn't want to do anything. She sleeps all day and stays out all night and steals money from her brother."

How many times had I heard similar sorrowful stories from mothers and fathers of wayward teens! The Blessed Virgin stressed continually in her messages at Medjugorje the importance of family and the power of family prayer. With prayer you can stop wars, she had said. The rampant drug addiction among young people is a dire warning of the need to stay in the battle with prayer. I told Veronica this and said that I would pray daily for her daughter. I found the situation frustrating: I wanted to do more to comfort the mother, but this was all I could do. At least, that is what I thought as I said good-bye to Veronica, not imagining that we would ever meet again. However, as the old cliché goes, God does indeed work in mysterious ways.

Upon returning home, Veronica told her daughter about our meeting and our talk at the church. Expecting the usual shrug and "that's cool" line of dismissal, she was surprised when Marie listened intently and then told her mother that she would like to meet me one day. The mother immediately sensed a little flicker of hope for the healing of her daughter and made a mental note that somehow, she would arrange this meeting sometime in the future.

The following winter a teenage friend of Marie's suddenly died from a drug overdose. He was only seventeen years old. Distraught and shaken, Marie attended his funeral service. For the first time, she realized her own susceptibility to such a fate. The bottom line to drug addiction was death.

One day in January 1999, out of the blue, a quiet, contrite Marie told her mother that she wanted to go to a church. . . . a church far from their home. She gave no explanation. Could this at last be a realization by Marie of her problem? Was the Virgin Mary finally responding to Veronica's ongoing prayers? When asked why she wanted to go to a church far away from home, Marie, eyes cast downward, said, "Mom, I can't go to our parish. I have too many friends there."

Within the hour, Veronica was driving her daughter to St. Benedict's Church in San Diego. She was taking no chances. Marie hated showing her weak and soft side, and the mother feared she would back out of her decision at any moment. But as soon as they entered the church, tears rolled down Marie's cheeks. At first it was soft sobbing. She tried to hide it, but soon she couldn't hide the tears that flowed down, washing away her eye makeup. She looked at her mother and sobbed, "Mom, I need your help."

Gratitude suddenly flooded Veronica's heart. The Blessed Mother had been listening to her prayers after all—and doing something about it. She saw the signs of return of her little Marie, of the sweet spirit in the contrition of her broken daughter. She would do whatever it would take to help her. But first, there was the need to confront the source of the problem.

Gently stroking her daughter's cheek, Veronica plunged ahead with a mother's love. "Marie, I love you and I will help you, but you are going to have to change some things. You need to get away from your addicted friends and those who are hanging out with them."

The mother's love had now taken full command, fueled by the impromptu collapse of Marie's wall of resistance to past attempts to help her. Emboldened, Veronica told Marie she needed to be far away from her present environment in order to accomplish a complete healing of her drug problem.

Later in the week, after many agonizing conversations, she convinced Marie to see a Korean doctor friend of the family. Both mother and daughter were taken aback when he firmly recommended a rehabilitation center in Korea. That meant separation from one another and from the entire family. Yet, deep in her heart, Veronica knew that the Blessed Virgin Mary was very much at work in this sudden breakthrough. Within the week, they flew to Korea to begin Marie's road to full recovery.

On Marie's arrival at the rehabilitation center, reality set in for her. She was confused and scared. "Mom, I can't do this," she told her mother. Veronica was doing her best to choke back tears and remain firm. "Yes, you can, Marie. Yes, you can!"

Veronica returned to the States, happy and sad at the same time. Mother and daughter began a routine of talking on the telephone once a week, as strongly suggested by the doctors at the center. Marie constantly asked to come home. The mother hid her tears of motherly compassion and reminded her daughter repeatedly that it would be only a temporary separation and they would "be together again soon." This was indeed tough mother's love.

Nearly four months would pass before Veronica and Marie were together again. Their reunion came about as a result of my going to Korea for approximately three weeks to give a series of talks on Medjugorje. In the mystery of what is often referred to as coincidence—renamed by followers of Medjugorje as "Godincidence"—I encountered Veronica again during the tour. She had purposely flown to Korea to meet with me.

It was soon evident to all of us that the mysterious ways of God were at work. I had met Charles and Bernadette Kim at a Marian conference in Irvine, California. Charles had contacted the organizers of the conference to request a meeting with me to offer his services for translating my books into the Korean language. I had readily agreed. In the process of working together, Charles and I became good friends, and in time, I further agreed to the speaking tour in Korea to publicize the newly translated books.

What I didn't know was that Bernadette and Charles were close friends of Veronica. They lived near each other and were members of the same Korean Catholic church. Bernadette had told Veronica that they were going to invite me to go to Korea for a series of talks. "Oh, I met him when he came here to give a talk on Medjugorje," she excitedly related to Bernadette. "Please, can you ask him if maybe he will meet with Marie at the rehabilitation center while he is in Korea?"

Bernadette did not hesitate to ask me if I would be willing to meet and speak with Marie at a predetermined time during the Korean tour. I readily agreed.

Several days into the tour, we met with an excited Veronica at the rehab center. I knew immediately that the meeting with Marie was as important as any aspect of the Korean tour. Once again, I experienced that inner nudging by the Blessed Virgin that I had felt so many times.

"Hi, I am so happy to finally meet you. Thank you for coming to see me!" With that warm greeting and a hug, I began a two-hour conversation with Veronica's daughter, Marie. While she was truly sincere and convinced that she was healed, it was immediately evident that she had her own agenda for meeting with me.

Veronica had explained to me in advance that she would not come into the meeting because Marie would begin begging to come home. "That is the main thing on her mind right now," she related. "She does not see that she is still not fully healed and that she needs to stay here."

The desperation soon came to the surface in my conversation with Marie. I was touched, and I left the meeting promising that I would tell her mother that maybe she would be better off at home.

"No, she is not ready," Veronica responded firmly when I began pleading Marie's case. "I would do anything to have my daughter back at home, but she will immediately go back to her old ways."

Six more months passed before Marie was able to leave the center. And when she did, Veronica insisted she stay on in Korea to attend school. In hindsight, the mother was right. It took the extra time in the center and then in Korea for Marie to find herself. She finally returned home appreciative of all that her mother had done for her.

To my delight, Veronica brought Marie, as well as her son John and several friends from their community, to Medjugorje as part of my pilgrimage group for the Youth Festival in 2000. It had been three years since Veronica had made that first pilgrimage to Medjugorje. She had left dejected that the Blessed Mother had not answered her pleas. Now, here we were again, this time with Marie. It was a joyful reunion for all of us.

But there was yet another twist to Marie's conversion story, one that I would find out later when interviewing her for the book. "I must tell you honestly," she said, "the healing and return to belief in God did not come in a flash of light; it wasn't immediate."

In fact, Marie went on to tell me, it was a roller-coaster ride of emotions. There were many temptations crossing her path as she was trying to break free from the death grasp of drugs. Drugs, she stated, were "like a Pandora's Box: Once you know the taste and its effect, it's hard to forget the euphoric feeling it temporarily brings."

There was one more thing she wanted to say, Marie told me. "I just want mothers and daughters alike to realize that patience and unconditional love are the key points; that even though the answer may not come when initially asked for . . . to never give up hope, because Our Lady never ignores and always answers."

Of course, Veronica knows that. Thanks to a mother's unwavering love, Marie is again a happy, sweet, beloved daughter, who also acknowledges the intercession of another Mother in her healing.

❧

"Dear children! I rejoice with you and in this time of grace I call you to spiritual renewal. Pray, little children, that the Holy Spirit may come to dwell in you in fullness, so that you may be able to witness in joy to all those who are far from faith. Especially, little children, pray for the gifts of the Holy Spirit so that in the spirit of love, every day and in each situation, you may be closer to your fellow-man; and that in wisdom and love you may overcome every difficulty. I am with you and I intercede for each of you before Jesus. Thank you for having responded to my call."

Monthly message given to the visionary Marija,
May 25, 2000.

THIRTEEN

"Ask and you will receive . . ."

In the years the Blessed Virgin Mary has appeared in apparition at Medjugorje, she has continually taught us to ask God through prayer for what we need. Her desire is that we focus on the spiritual graces of prayer, fasting, and penance. But this does not exclude asking for material goods necessary for daily living. A young lady named Marian discovered this as she prepared to leave on pilgrimage to Medjugorje after graduating from high school.

Marian was a brilliant, dedicated student, graduating from high school with top honors. She would be attending a high-level university on full scholarship in the fall. This was fortunate for Marian, because her family was unable to pay the high tuition costs for her continuing studies. Even though she was the only child, expenses were tight due to heavy medical bills brought on by the frail health of her mother.

Marian's father was a devout man who gave his family much in the way of spiritual needs. He had managed to save enough over the years to give his daughter a special graduation gift. His intent was to buy her a modest, but dependable used car, so that she could travel between home and school when possible, since the university was located a good six hours away. Marian had dreamed for years of one day owning her own car.

That had been the plan—until their little family discovered Medjugorje just before Marian was due to graduate from high school.

The family learned about Medjugorje for the first time in depth after attending a Marian conference in a nearby city. Marian's father had always had a strong love for the Blessed Mother, as he called her, but knew little about her apparitions in Medjugorje before the conference. Now he was on fire. His daughter was even more on fire. "I would love to go there more than anything," she said wistfully, as they drove home from the conference.

Her father drove on in silence, nodding his head to show his understanding. He wished that *he* could go and take his wife, and ask the Blessed Mother to intercede for a healing for her. As his wife and daughter excitedly chatted on about the happenings at the conference, an idea began to form. Maybe there was a way. But it would be a decision for his daughter to make. "Marian," he began slowly, "there might be a way for you to go to Medjugorje, but it will take a sacrifice on your part—and on ours."

Marian was stunned. "What do you mean?"

Her father waited a moment. "Well, you can have your car as a graduation present as we planned, or. . . ."

Marian knew exactly what her father meant: She could go to Medjugorje, but she would have to choose between going to Medjugorje and owning a car. Not having a car meant that she could not come home from school before the end of each semester, and her father would have to drive her to school and come pick her up. It would be a hardship for all of them.

"Medjugorje," she answered quietly with a half smile. "I know it sounds crazy, and we just learned about it, but there's something inside calling me there." The decision was made on the spur of the moment after months of thinking and planning for the day she would own her own car.

A week later, Marian and her parents had made all of the arrangements. She would be in Medjugorje for the Youth Festival in August. They celebrated that evening by attending a special fund-raiser at their church to help the poor and the homeless.

As they wandered through the church hall, Marian came to a stop at a table offering raffle tickets for $100 each on a brand-new car. "Hey, there you go," her Dad said jokingly. "Buy one of these and you can go to Medjugorje *and* have a car!"

Marian looked at her father. "Dad, would you get one for me? I'll pay you back when we get home."

"Are you sure?" he asked, knowing she was serious. "That's a lot of money."

"I've saved some money from my part-time jobs, and this is for a real good cause." Marian paused a moment. "Oh, I'd like to win the car, but that's not the main thing."

With that, Marian's father took out his credit card and purchased a ticket for his daughter.

"Yes, in every way possible. It was awesome," Marian answered softly, when her dad asked her if her decision to go to Medjugorje instead of having her own car was worth it. They had been home from the airport only a short time, and Marian had not stopped talking about her experience in the village since her father had picked her up. Looking a bit sheepish, she added, "I must admit, I did pray to Our Lady on Apparition Hill that it would be nice if I won that car in the raffle."

"Well, you must have asked in the right way," he answered, having hardly been able to contain himself ever since picking her up at the airport. "Because you did win. You now own a brand-new car!"

❧

"Dear children: I ask you to pray and give your life completely to God. I will give you strength in all of your needs. You can ask for what you want. I can give it to you. I will intercede for you to the Father."

Given to the visionary Marija
at Caritas of Birmingham in Birmingham, Alabama,
on November 23, 1988.

FOURTEEN

Brian: "I will protect you . . ."

There is a point and time in life when many people discover the reality of God. It is a singular moment that marks the start of true spiritual conversion through acceptance of that reality. For people of all ages coming to Medjugorje, it is the overriding grace of the apparitions that brings the reality into sharp focus. And while many discover the reality of God in their teens, far too many people do not experience it until something dramatic happens in their life to focus them on the reality.

For eighteen-year-old Brian, the reality came upon him gradually in his early teen years. But it was at Medjugorje that it changed noticeably from parental influence and obligation, to a personal desire to be part of it. He came to Medjugorje as a member of my youth festival pilgrimage in August 2001, gleaning a treasure lode of memories from the pilgrimage.

Brian felt that something special happened to him during his pilgrimage to Medjugorje. However, it would take a second dramatic event a month later to make the discovery of the reality of God an unforgettable and permanent part of his daily life. It occurred on September 8, 2001, the day the Church celebrates the birthday of the Blessed Virgin Mary.

On this hot, muggy day, after trying to find some friends to go with him, Brian decided to go target shooting in the woods alone. He practiced for a while, but it wasn't as much fun as when his friends were with him. After a while, he decided to give up and go home.

As he was putting his gun away, the gun accidentally discharged, shooting Brian in the right thigh. Filled with sudden pain and the realization that he had shot himself, he blacked out. When he came to, he began hopping on one leg to try to get back out of the woods to get help.

It was not long before Brian noticed he was bleeding so profusely that his jeans were soaked in blood. How did this happen, he questioned himself? He had always handled guns carefully and had taken safety training to ensure that such a thing could not happen. But it had, and now here he was in a mess.

Brian's mind was spinning but still able to reason, even though fear and panic were close at hand. He at least knew that he had to get out of the woods fast and find help. He at least knew that, despite the fact that his consciousness was fading in and out. But each time Brian tried to stand up, he fell again. He removed his shirt and tried to make a tourniquet for his leg with it as he had been taught, but it would not work because his leg was too swollen.

Before long, Brian was unable to walk and fell to the ground. He began crawling on his belly. Soon he became dehydrated. He crawled toward the nearest of several large, muddy puddles of rainwater left from the previous day's storm and sipped from it. By this time, the stagnant water tasted good.

But Brian's senses were fading more now and his breathing became labored. As he began crawling from puddle to puddle, he weakly screamed for help. But there didn't seem to be another soul in the woods that day. After a while, he lost track of time.

At some point, the wounded young man regained consciousness long enough to remember a very important thing:

He had a rosary from Medjugorje in his pocket. He reached in and took out the wooden rosary, wrapped it around the fingers of his left hand and crawled to the next puddle. One thought kept running through Brian's mind. He had learned how to truly pray with his heart while in Medjugorje, to ask for Our Lady's help in all situations. There was no better time than now. "Blessed Mary, please help me," he prayed weakly, clutching the rosary to his chest.

As he rested on his back in one of the puddles, Brian started to relax. Dragging himself from puddle to puddle, he continued to pray, "Hail Mary, full of grace . . ." Finally he reached what looked to be the last one, larger and deeper than what he had already been through. In front of him was a big hill. He made himself as comfortable as possible in the water and prepared to die.

Brian closed his eyes and continued to pray, "Hail Mary, full of grace . . ." and then, as he felt himself losing consciousness possibly for the last time, "Dear Mother of God, help me!"

After what seemed to be hours of lying there, slowly feeling the life ebbing out of him, Brian thought he heard the noise of motors. With what little strength he had left after having crawled approximately 500 yards, he again yelled for help. Suddenly, two men on all-terrain vehicles arrived and immediately inquired if he was all right. And while he could not answer the men right away, Brian sensed that his prayers to the Blessed Virgin Mary had been heard—and answered. The words of her message he remembered hearing at Medjugorje kept repeating in his mind: *"I will protect you!"*

The men didn't realize at first that Brian was suffering from the gunshot wound. He was not bleeding anymore, as he was virtually out of blood. He told them that he had accidentally shot himself. As they tried to make him comfortable, one of the men casually asked him, trying to relax him a bit more, "What's that in your hand, son?"

Barely able to breathe, much less speak, Brian answered, "My rosary."

Within the hour, the two men helped Brian onto one of the ATVs and drove him to the nearest house, where they called 911. He was immediately taken to the hospital, where it was discovered that he had severed a major artery in his thigh, and would have to have bypass surgery to repair it. Amazingly, the bullet had exited the leg through the back and had not done any damage to the bone, surrounding muscle, or major nerves.

The next day, a policeman came to the hospital to complete the report of the accident. "You're a lucky young man," he told Brian. "If those men had not found you when they did, you might not have made it." If they had gone for help and then come back, he continued, it would have been too late.

When the policeman later gave the names of the men on the four-wheelers to Brian and his parents, they called them right away to thank them. Both men humbly admitted that it was God who had saved Brian, and that they had just been in the right place at the right time. They told him that they had not been planning on going four-wheeling that day, but only went because of a chance of rain the following day. They also related that they almost never go to that part of the woods, and had not been there in months.

Adding to the collection of astounding details; even with their helmets on the men were able to hear Brian's cries for help over their loud motors, and where they found Brian was the exact opposite direction of the way Brian had intended to go. He had been disoriented as he had faded in and out of consciousness. Brian was surprised that they were able to see him at all, as his whole body, except for his head, had become immersed in the deep puddle.

❦

To Brian's accident and rescue there is a footnote that is just as miraculous as the story itself. The day after Brian was rescued, his father, who is a U.S. Army Reserve criminal investigator, went into the woods to follow the path where Brian crawled. He took photographs of the scene. As he was showing the photos at the hospital, someone noticed that in the mud where Brian crawled with his rosary were images that resembled Jesus and the Blessed Virgin Mary. In Our Lady's image, she seemed to be holding a rosary.

The incidence of the pictures was just more proof to Brian that she was there with him to protect him as she promised through her messages at Medjugorje. Still, the greatest realization for him was that God, indeed, was real.

His life would never be the same.

❦

"Dear children: I need your prayers, now more than ever before. I beseech you to take your rosary in your hands, now, more than ever before. Grasp it strongly, and pray with all your heart in these difficult times. Thank you for having gathered in such a number and for having responded to my call."

Message given to the visionary Mirjana
on her birthday, March 18, 1992.

FIFTEEN

The day the earth shook in Medjugorje!

It was Thursday, the first morning of talks for the 2003 Youth Festival at Medjugorje. The weather was hot but not overbearing as it had been the previous week, when temperatures had reached more than 100 degrees.

It didn't matter to the young people. They had come from more than forty countries from around the world. For this special festival I had a group of forty pilgrims, most of them teenagers.

We had difficulty getting to Medjugorje; there were delays in flights, lost luggage, and even a breakdown of one of the smaller buses on the tedious three-hour journey from Dubrovnik to Medjugorje. Hungry and worn to exhaustion, we arrived about 10 PM on Wednesday night. After a quick meal we fell into our beds for a short sleep before getting up to begin the pilgrimage at 7 AM. Attesting to the wondrous energy of youth, there were few complaints.

On the morning the festival began, young people filled the benches and spaces surrounding the outside altar area behind St. James Church. There were Chinese young people from Hong Kong and young Palestinians from Israel, and eleven teenagers from Ukraine; they were all the first pilgrims to Medjugorje from their countries.

As the opening day talks commenced, Medjugorje was transformed once again into a sea of chanting, singing, dancing, happy teenagers. Right away, the audience was revved up by an hour-long prelude of prayers and snappy, upbeat religious music. This was the living fulfillment of the dream that the late Father Slavko Barbaric had had when he began working non-stop to create the annual Youth Festival at Medjugorje. And this year would offer a startling exclamation point to his dream come true.

The opening talks had set the tone for the festival. The last speaker of the morning was a highly charismatic Croatian Franciscan priest, who immediately increased the level of intensity by honing in on the core of the conference theme: the belief in and the love of Jesus.

"Do you believe in Jesus?" he asked the crowd, repeating his question a number of times when the young people did not respond as fully as he would have liked. He continued one last time, quoting from a line of Scripture that he had quoted earlier, which read, "For the windows of heaven are opened, and the foundations of the earth tremble" (Isaiah 24:18b).

"If you *really* believe in Jesus," he trumpeted after quoting the Scripture verse again, "then the earth will truly shake!"

Finally, there came the response he wanted—a thunderous, *"Yes! We believe!"*

Now, with the young people at maximum attentiveness, he proclaimed, "If you believe, if you really believe, then stand up right now and shout, 'I believe in Jesus!' . . . *and the earth will be shaken!"*

The crowd of more than 3,000 young people rose as one and began shouting, "I believe in Jesus! I believe in Jesus!"

On that emotional note, the youth festival broke at noon for lunch. Hardly had most of the young people settled down for their meal, buzzing with conversation about the last speaker of the morning, when suddenly there was a deep rumble, and the ground and the buildings began literally to shake and sway. An earthquake lasting more than four seconds shook the holy shrine of Medjugorje and all of its inhabitants and pilgrims!

The words of the Franciscan priest—"If you really believe in Jesus, then the earth will shake!"—sprang into the minds of all who had been there that morning.

"Dear children! God gives me this time as a gift to you, so that I may instruct and lead you on the path of salvation. Dear children, now you do not comprehend this grace, but soon a time will come when you will lament for these messages. That is why, little children, live all of the words which I have given you through this time of grace and renew prayer, until prayer becomes a joy for you. Especially, I call all those who have consecrated themselves to my Immaculate Heart to become an example to others. I call all priests and religious brothers and sisters to pray the rosary and to teach others to pray. The rosary, little children, is especially dear to me. Through the rosary open your heart to me and I am able to help you. Thank you for having responded to my call."

Monthly message given to the visionary Marija,
August 25, 1997.

SIXTEEN

Josh and Andrea: A Medjugorje love story

Clearly, the messages given by the Blessed Virgin Mary at Medjugorje emphasize the love God has for His children. When we are young, we are nourished by that grace and are dependent on it and protected by it. It is all we know. Then we reach the age of reason where we consciously know right from wrong. This is a crossroads of life when many children begin to lose the unconditional holy love of innocence.

Too often there is one thing that causes the loss of that innocence. The result creates dark misery in a young life that is nearly impossible to overcome.

There are countless stories of young people living in this dark misery who come to Medjugorje and rediscover God's grace. They are classic repeats of the parable of the prodigal son found in Holy Scripture—like the story of Goran described in an earlier chapter. Like Goran, some receive a special, additional grace: They find a person with whom they can share their rekindled love of God forever.

This is the story of two such "prodigals" who rediscovered God's grace through pilgrimage to the little village, and in the process found each other. It is a true Medjugorje love story.

First, Josh's story:

In the summer of 2000 Josh was invited by his mother to go with her on a pilgrimage to Medjugorje, but Josh wasn't sure.

He wanted to go and needed to go, but he had just been through nearly five years in a dark, murky state with no real love of God or neighbor or church. It had been five years marked by dependence on alcohol and drugs, and a disastrous relationship with a girl he had lived with but had no intention of marrying. This was the second such relationship, coming on the heels of a painful divorce in 1997 from the mother of his only child, a little girl.

His adult life had started so promising. After finishing school, Josh had gone to work for the family business, fulfilling a lifelong dream of his father to work with his sons. Josh had a twin brother, Joel, who had taken the path of misery at a younger age and was steeped in drugs and alcohol. Joel's misery had already broken the father's heart many times.

The dream of at least one son working with him lasted only a short time. Josh stayed briefly, left, and returned for another short stay before leaving a second time—again breaking the father's heart.

The confused young man hastily married but soon found he had made a mistake. When the marriage ended in divorce, Josh only made his life worse. Like his brother Joel, he began to drink heavily, using the breakup of his family as an easy excuse. Indulgence in drugs was the next step. With dependence on his addictions came a slackening of responsibility. For the poor parents, two sons were now living in dark misery.

The one-time altar boy was no longer the good son to his parents or the caring father he should have been to his little girl. Josh saw little of his parents, and he had visiting privileges with his daughter only every other weekend. All of his misfortune he blamed on his former wife.

The spiritually broken young man began working at a factory earning a decent living. But the expense of his addictions was more than he was earning, creating yet another problem. Adding to the misery, Josh was twice arrested for driving under the influence of alcohol, and his license was suspended for a minimum of five years.

Now, five years later, after losing his job at the factory for missing work far too often due to long nights of partying and drugs, Josh, the prodigal son, was home. He found a loving, forgiving father and mother who were delighted to have him back, and once again he started working for the family business.

The invitation from his mother to go to Medjugorje reawakened good childhood memories for Josh. Deep in his heart, he knew he should have sought help from the Church a long time ago. But reliance and trust in the Church was a thing of the past. The only times in the last five years he had gone to church were at Christmas and Easter. He had been raised with a knowledge and respect for the church sacraments and had attended Catholic grade school for seven years. Then something happened that changed everything.

Josh claimed that he was abused by the priest in his parish.

It was because of the claimed abuse that Josh no longer wanted to go to church. This was, in hindsight, the impetus for the devastating change in behavior that led to his misery.

In spite of his problems, Josh had always looked up to his mother. They had a special relationship, one that allowed her a little more leeway and control than others had with him. Now that he was back with the family, she started "working" on him.

When she had first asked him to go to Medjugorje with her in 1999, along with his twin brother, Joel, and her sister Donna, who had been diagnosed with lung cancer a year earlier, he declined. But surprising himself, he was anxious for them to return so that he could learn more about this place where the Blessed Virgin was reportedly appearing.

When they did return, Josh could see that the experience had made a strong impression on his brother, Joel. His eyes were clear, having had time to recover from chronic use of drugs and alcohol. He also was smiling a lot. Joel felt he had been healed in his own way, and his personal accounts of the pilgrimage amazed Josh to the point that he felt he had to go there as well.

Regrettably for Joel, he was surrounded by weak peers who could only mock his experience. Shortly after his return home from Medjugorje, Joel went back to drinking and drugs and to infrequent visits with his family. He became an unfortunate example of the seed described in the parable of the seed in Scripture, seed that falls into shallow soil to sprout for a limited time before dying off. Even in his own failure, it was painful for Josh to see his brother return to his dark days.

Now his mother was again asking Josh to go to Medjugorje with her. It would be just the two of them. After a momentary hesitation and reflection on his life to this point, Josh accepted his mother's invitation. He suddenly realized how much he had missed the relationship with his parents, and how bad a personal relationship he had with yet another girl at this time. That relationship was lacking in substance, and both Josh and his girlfriend knew it.

After several days of deep and sometimes contentious discussion about Josh's upcoming trip to Medjugorje, his girlfriend was hoping he would come back changed and everything would be how it was when they had first met. But Josh had a totally different outlook. He had a premonition the day he left for Medjugorje that the relationship was over.

❦

The pilgrimage to several religious sites in Italy and then on to Medjugorje was to start on May 18. Josh and his mother drove to St. Louis and waited for the rest of the group to show up for the flight to New York. When the group was together at the gate awaiting the flight, Josh noticed an exceptionally attractive young lady about his age there with her mother. He felt an immediate attraction. But just as quickly he checked it; the last thing he needed, he thought, was to pursue another relationship. Yet, he couldn't stop looking at her or thinking about her.

It was during the first overseas stop of the pilgrimage that Josh found the courage to approach the attractive young woman. He gave the usual "Hi, how are you, where are you from" greeting, and that was it. The two exchanged names and began conversation. After that, Josh found himself drawn to wherever Andrea happened to be. They were conversing in brief spurts, but the spurts were becoming frequent.

The group arrived in Assisi, Italy, the famous home of St. Francis, the first stop of the Italian tour before going on to Medjugorje. Josh finally got up the nerve to ask Andrea's mother if it might be all right if he and Andrea had a glass of wine together. He was delighted when Andrea's mother said it was fine. Andrea was impressed with his gentlemanly approach.

They stayed up in the lounge of the hotel with a few other young people, talking and watching local soccer on television. Later, they went to a cathedral across the street to hear Gregorian chant. Josh and Andrea were awestruck by the beautiful singing—and with each other.

Several tour stops later, two mothers were concerned: Josh and Andrea were now constantly together. Thinking of each child's past mistakes, the mothers feared the two young people were getting too serious too quickly. Josh's mother pulled him aside, explaining that she did not want the friendship between Josh and Andrea to ruin the tour experience and take away from the impact of the wonderful sites they were seeing. Josh assured his mother that there was nothing to worry about. Memories of past and present relationships were still fresh in his thoughts. Besides, he reminded his mother, it was she who had told him to find someone he could be comfortable with spiritually, and that maybe he would find that person during this pilgrimage. What mother and son did not realize was that he had already found the person he was looking for.

The group finished the Italian part of the spiritual tour and boarded a ferry for the eight-hour crossing of the Adriatic Sea to the port of Ancona. From there they would travel by bus through Croatia and into Bosnia-Hercegovina, where Medjugorje was located.

It was a fateful crossing for Josh and Andrea. Sleep was forgotten as they poured out their hearts to each other. Josh told Andrea about all of his dismal "baggage" of the last five years, and she, in turn did the same to him. They just talked and enjoyed each other's company. This was a first for Josh. He was sharing intimate thoughts with a beautiful young woman without feeling like he had to have sex with her, or that there was any pressure to do anything but share thoughts with each other.

In spite of being riveted by his time with Andrea, Josh was overwhelmed by Medjugorje. He went to confession on their first full day there, a confession like never before in his life. It was the pivotal point in his return to the security of the love of God.

Coming out of the confessional, Josh grabbed his mother. "Mom, we've got to talk," he said, and they started walking. He broke into tears and began to apologize to her for all the grief and anguish he had put her through, and for not being the son to her and his dad and the father to his daughter. They walked, talked, and cried together. When the walk was over, Josh was finally at peace.

Josh and Andrea were staying in separate homes in Medjugorje. Yet, he was at her house every morning, waiting for her to come down the stairs. They spent hours together at the Blue Cross, a special place near the bottom of Podbrdo Hill where Our Lady had appeared numerous times to the visionary Ivan and his prayer group. It became their special place in Medjugorje.

One evening the young couple was there with Ivan and his group during an apparition. Suddenly, Andrea began to cry. "What's wrong?" Josh whispered.

Andrea looked at him. "Can you see anything in the moon?" she asked.

Josh looked and then quietly answered, "Yes, I can see the Blessed Mother's face in the moon." Andrea told him that she, too, could see it. Afterward, they walked the streets for hours, just talking and being together.

Several days later the group drove twenty-five miles to the parish of Siroki Brijeg to see Father Jozo, the charismatic priest who was the pastor at Medjugorje when the apparitions started in June 1981. Father Jozo is blessed with many gifts of the Holy Spirit, and a stop at his present parish is an inevitable part of almost all pilgrimages to Medjugorje.

When Father Jozo prayed over Josh and Andrea, they were both "slain" in the spirit, a state of complete rest in the Holy Spirit of God. This anointing became a sign to them that they were meant to be together.

On the bus ride home from Siroki Brijeg, it seemed that most of the group kept staring at them, as, according to Josh's mother later, the young couple was actually glowing from the experience.

After two years of long-distance courtship—Josh lived in Illinois and Andrea lived in Kansas—they were married in May 2003, two years to the week they first met in Medjugorje.

Upon returning home from that fateful pilgrimage to Medjugorje, Josh confirmed his conversion in his own mind. He was at last able to forgive the priest he claimed had sexually abused him. He would come to understand that forgiveness of others, and forgiveness of self, is the real key to conversion. The love for—and from—his new bride, Andrea, had much to do with it.

The prodigal son had fully returned.

"Dear children! Do not forget that you are here on earth on the way to eternity and that your home is in heaven. That is why, little children, be open to God's love and leave egoism and sin. May your joy be only in discovering God in daily prayer. That is why, make good use of this time and pray, pray, pray; and God is near to you in prayer and through prayer. Thank you for having responded to my call."

Monthly message given to the visionary Marija,
July 25, 2000.

SEVENTEEN

Josh and Andrea: Part II

Andrea's story:

Despite a happy childhood surrounded by a loving, supportive family steeped in the teachings of the Catholic Church, Andrea had become a rebellious teenager. At age eighteen, she found herself pregnant and alone.

After painfully admitting her guilt and consulting with her parents, Andrea decided to put her newborn daughter up for adoption. In her frightened, immature state, this was the only way she felt she could cope; the only way to right the wrong she had created. She could not bear the thought of being a single mother, leaving her daughter with no father.

The father disappeared immediately after Andrea disclosed to him that she was pregnant. She thought she was in love with him and that he loved her; surely he would do the right thing and marry her. After his disappearance, she knew better. She would say later, "When I gave up my daughter, I felt as though I gave up my soul."

The trauma of becoming pregnant and then giving up her baby left Andrea empty and with the constant guilt of what she had done. She had truly wanted to be a responsible mother more than anything in the world. She wanted a husband who felt the same way. However, she knew deep inside that she was not mentally, physically, or spiritually prepared for the all-consuming task of motherhood by herself.

Slowly, as the months passed, Andrea was drawn back to her faith, but still lacked a real commitment. There was so much living to do as a teenager, and it helped cover the memory of her trauma. She did her best to forget the past and settle into a daily life of study and fun at college.

It was during her sophomore year in college that her mother approached Andrea about going to Medjugorje. She excitedly told her daughter about the Blessed Mother appearing there every day and of the miraculous healings that were taking place. Despite her mother's enthusiasm, Andrea was slow to accept, finally agreeing to go, more to please her mother than for herself. It would be a good thing to do, she rationalized: Her mother wanted her to go; besides, her brother would also be going.

Andrea's initial reluctance to go on the pilgrimage was primarily because of a new boyfriend. She seemed to be constantly looking for "Mr. Right," but this relationship wasn't going well. There were too many memories of the hurt and loss from the last time. She sensed that if she went on this trip, her relationship with the new boyfriend would be over.

There was something else. Andrea had a feeling that she was actually being called to this place of miracles, as if an inner voice were saying, "Come to Medjugorje. . . ."

"Okay, I'll go," Andrea had finally said to her mother. And then, making light of it to cover the tingling she felt with the inner urge, she added, "Hey, it's a trip to another country, so why not?"

Andrea had no real idea what Medjugorje was about despite her mother's attempts to tell her. Outwardly, she acted as excited as she could for her mother's sake, but inwardly, she was just "along for the ride"—except for that inner voice, and until she noticed Josh in the airport in New York.

Andrea felt the same attraction to Josh as he did to her, but she didn't want to be hurt again. She wanted nothing to do with another close relationship with a man. Deep down in her soul, though, there was a stirring. Her desire to marry the man of her dreams, one who wouldn't run away from responsibility, one who wanted children as much as she did, was still very much alive.

There was small talk between them, and Andrea took notice that Josh seemed to be sincere and kind. When Josh asked her mother for permission to have a glass of wine with her in Assisi, her heart leapt, but she had no expectations. They talked a little more in depth and began to get to know each other.

Little by little, Andrea became more open to the religious side of the trip. She would later say she felt the Holy Spirit working on her with each holy place they visited. Her heart was being worked on, being opened to the Blessed Mother—and to Josh, who seemed to be around everywhere they went on the tour. They soon were spending most of the tour side by side.

Once in Medjugorje, Josh and Andrea stayed up until the wee hours of the morning just talking, sharing experiences and thoughts. Before long, Andrea knew that this bond was extremely special. Her fears were forgotten while she was with Josh. They prayed the Rosary together at the Blue Cross and experienced all of the unique, "magical," and indescribable experiences and feelings of Medjugorje together. Without either of them knowing it, they had found that special person each was seeking.

Having heard Josh's side of the story related in the previous chapter, Andrea put it this way: "The most amazing moments were the miracles we experienced. We witnessed the sun "dancing" and smelled the scent of roses. And most special was an evening of song and prayer while we looked on while one of the visionaries had an apparition."

And of course, there was the special sign for Josh and Andrea during that evening when they were present for the apparition at the Blue Cross. Andrea said, "I looked up and the moon was bright and beautiful. As I looked I saw the Blessed Mother as clear as can be in the moon. I knew people experienced amazing phenomena there but I had never expected such a blessing. I had prayed, 'Please give me a sign, and show me, I want to see you.' I just wasn't 'feeling it' to the extent I was now longing for.

"As I cried, I asked Josh if he saw anything. When he replied yes, I asked if he thought it was a face in the moon. He replied it was the Blessed Mother, and we wept and wept and said Hail Marys in thanksgiving for the amazing blessing we were given. I couldn't believe we were experiencing this together, and I knew this man was special."

From that point, Josh and Andrea grew so close it was as though they had known each other for years. The other pilgrims from their group joked and teased the two of them about being together all the time. Their mothers no longer worried about them. If the Blessed Mother wanted them together, the mothers reasoned, they would be together!

Andrea tried to remain cautious, even though caution was in total contradiction to what she truly felt inside her heart. She simply could not believe that she had finally found that one special person of her dreams. As they were saying their good-byes after arriving in New York, Josh gave Andrea a warm and tender hug like she had never experienced. He then gave her a letter, telling her to read it when she was on the plane heading home.

Once in the air on the final leg of their journey, Andrea opened Josh's letter. He wrote that no matter what or where their lives went from there, with the spiritual connection they had discovered at Medjugorje, they had to keep in touch and remain friends. She truly wanted that too.

Josh telephoned Andrea's home before she arrived from the airport, leaving her a message. She didn't return the call. Could this really be happening? she thought. Was he really the one? Before she had time to think further, the telephone rang. It was Josh—again!

In the following days, all of the defenses were down for Andrea. Josh was so easy to fall in love with. They talked on the phone or e-mailed daily and visited each other when they could for the next two years until they were finally married.

❦

There was concern in both families that a long-distance relationship wouldn't make it, but when God is behind a relationship, everything is possible. It all seemed to fall into place. For the first time, Andrea's parents approved of the man she was with.

The marriage took place two years to the day of their pilgrimage, and the priest who had served as spiritual director for the trip performed the ceremony. Andrea would later say that the Blessed Mother "gave me my heart's desire of my dream wedding and the husband God meant for me along with the healing I so desperately needed, emotionally and spiritually." Andrea found out later that when she gave birth to her daughter, her mother had prayed that within two years, she would find her true husband.

As of the completion of this book, Andrea and Josh have not been able to conceive a child. Yet, in true faith and trust in God, they have their children's names chosen—inspired, they say, by the enormous blessings of their pilgrimage. The names they have selected are Mariana, Christiana, Elijah Eric, and Garrett Matthew.

This wonderful Medjugorje love story is further proof that no one can go to Medjugorje and not have their life changed and blessed in unimaginable ways. Josh and Andrea long to return to Medjugorje. They will wait, knowing the Blessed Mother will one day call them back.

"Dear children! Today I rejoice with your patron saint and call you to be open to God's will, so that in you and through you, faith may grow in the people you meet in your everyday life. Little children, pray until prayer becomes joy for you. Ask your holy protectors to help you grow in love towards God. Thank you for having responded to my call."

Monthly message given to the visionary Marija,
July 25, 2002.

EIGHTEEN

The penance of love

In an earlier chapter we spoke of prayer, fasting, and penance as the cornerstones of the Medjugorje message. Penance is seemingly the least understood. But simply put, penance is service to our brothers and sisters in Christ. That is why I call it a penance of love.

Many young people on my trips to Medjugorje for the Youth Festival discover the penance of love when we visit a close-by refugee camp. The horrible civil war that took place in former Yugoslavia from 1991 into 1994 left 300,000 people dead. Among those killed were nearly 100,000 women and children. Ten of thousands more were left orphaned, homeless, and hopeless, living desperate lives in squalid surroundings.

The camp we visit shocks our young pilgrims when they see their peers living in such conditions. The refugees live in small aluminum huts that are like furnaces in the summer and refrigerators in the winter. There is one large bathroom and one large kitchen to be shared by all.

As peace returned to the region following the war, I became active in a charity named "Rebuild for Bosnia" in the fall of 1999. The purpose of the charity is to provide housing for the most desperate of refugee families. We began to place families in prefabricated homes wherever we could secure enough land in and around Medjugorje. Many of the families we placed in homes came from the refugee camp.

The goal in taking the young people on our Youth Festival trips to the camp is to allow them to see how spending time with these brothers and sisters in Christ is a precious gift of dignity. We also help the refugees with basic articles of clothing and cash donations for food and medicine. Every pilgrim who comes on my tours is asked to bring these articles with them as gifts for the refugees.

On a recent Youth Festival pilgrimage, I encountered a rarity: unruly, somewhat rebellious teenagers amongst our teens. Two boys in particular were determined to do things their way regardless of the requests of family members, our local guide Slavenka, and me. Their little acts of immaturity had already caused minor embarrassment to the family members who had brought them, and to our other pilgrims. I was mostly concerned about their overall influence on the other young people on the tour.

One young man, sixteen-year-old Brad, seemed bent on causing trouble. Shortly after members of the group had settled into their rooms, we milled around the front yard of our pilgrim house awaiting the evening meal. Brad, dressed in baggy jeans and shirt, his hair done in thick gel and ears sporting heavy metal earrings, approached me. "What do you think about smoking marijuana?" he asked outright, and then answered his own question: "I think it's cool and there's nothing wrong with it."

I looked at him for a moment. "Why do you feel you need to use a drug to be cool?"

He smiled, confident now that he had gained my attention. "So that I can feel good. Like I said, it's cool and it should be legal."

"Well, it's *not* legal and if you're really cool, you shouldn't need anything to make you feel good. Maybe that's why you're in Medjugorje, which I hope will help you to see that."

"Aw, man, I've been here one time before for all that religious stuff," Brad responded with a smirk. "This time I just want to have a good time."

Clinging to what little patience I had left, I smiled and walked away without responding further.

But Brad was not finished. He approached Slavenka. "Hey, you live here, right? Where can I find some good grass?"

Slavenka, who has been my guide for nearly all of my Youth Festival pilgrimage, and who speaks fluent English including most slang, looked young Brad directly in the eye. "Well," she smiled, "just look down at your feet and all around you here. You can see there is plenty of grass for you."

"Come on, you know what I mean. I want weed, marijuana, some good stuff."

Slavenka hesitated for a few moments. Without changing her smiling demeanor, she said quietly, "You know, you are not behaving too well." With that, she walked away.

Then there was Joey. Joey was a strapping teen who liked to kid around. He, too, would make outrageous comments just to see the shock value on adult faces and to impress the other teens. He refused to attend Mass despite the pleadings of his aunt, who had spent her own money to bring him to Medjugorje, in the hope that it would transform him. Neither Joey nor Brad attended Mass or the festival events during the first several days of the tour. Instead they spent hours at the large swimming facility on the outskirts of the village, or in the cafés eating pizza and joking around.

There, in the example of these two young men, is the classic and most common usage of the penance of love. It is to accept others as they are, regardless of our personal judgment or dislike, and to help them even when to do so is uncomfortable.

With only a couple days left on the tour, I scheduled a short afternoon trip to the refugee camp. We would take all of the goods brought by the group and visit with the refugees for an hour before returning to Medjugorje for the evening services. Surprisingly, without argument Joey and Brad agreed to come along.

The sixteen-mile trip to the camp by bus was a good time to tell the group about the war and the situation of the refugees. As always, Slavenka did an admirable job, speaking in a clear, rhythmic tone and giving accounts of what went on during the worst days of the war. Buildings along the way still bore the scourge of thousands of bullets and shells, while rebuilt structures served as silent testimony of the devastation that had taken place.

When Slavenka finished, I took the mic briefly to tell the group what to expect. "Please bear in mind," I began, "these people were living daily, normal lives just as you do at home. Suddenly they found themselves evicted, family members killed, and no place to go, and an enemy army ruling over them. Our purpose in coming here is just to spend time with them to let them know we care. . . ."

Within minutes following my words a collection for food and medicine was started, and I was given in excess of $600 to give to Ivanka, the camp supervisor.

There was not much more to say other than to ask them to try to keep their emotions in check while with the refugees. And they did so as much as possible. But many of the young people—including Brad and Joey—were visibly stunned as we mingled with the crowds of the camp, who were all too happy to have a momentary break from the daily drudgery of involuntary community living. The kids quickly joined in helping to move the goods we had brought to a storage area.

Now, they were living the other classic example of the penance of love: to do for others out of personal compassion.

Several of the young people living in the camp spoke English, and before long, impromptu invitations were issued for our young people and other pilgrims to briefly visit families inside the aluminum huts where they lived. The kids saw the living conditions, the community kitchen, and the toilet facilities, and the reality of the refugees' plight began to sink in.

As our bus pulled away from the camp about an hour later, there was silence on the bus until Slavenka suggested we pray a Rosary. It was the only conversation until our arrival back in Medjugorje.

That evening, I saw both Joey and Brad at the Rosary service, and they stayed for the Croatian Mass. There was no more talk from Brad about "grass." Joey was quieter than usual at dinner late that night at our pilgrim house. After dinner, several of the young people approached me. "Mr. Weible, we were just wondering if we can go back to that camp tomorrow with some more food and stuff."

And they did. They hired a taxi van and driver, went to the nearby grocery store, and loaded up with goods to take to the camp. Brad joined them, taking the last place in the van.

Joey came up to me just before the van was to leave. He reached into his pocket and took out a twenty-dollar bill. "Here," he said, "tell them to give this to the lady that runs that camp—it's all I have left."

It was evident among *all* of our young pilgrims that the penance of love had registered.

"Dear children, today I thank you for your prayers. You all have helped me so that this war may finish as soon as possible. I am close to you and I pray for each one of you and I beg you, pray, pray, pray. Only through prayer we can defeat evil and protect all that which Satan wants to destroy in your life. I am your Mother and I love you all the same, and I intercede for you before God. Thank you for having responded to my call."

Message given to the visionary Marija,
February 25, 1994.

NINETEEN

Michelle: The little cross

Until baby Michelle was fourteen months old, she appeared to be healthy and developmentally normal, just like her twin sister, Kristin. She could walk and run, sing and play like any toddler her age. But then there came a sudden change in her health that left her with a terminal health condition, and her family with an almost unbearable cross.

In November 1998, Michelle developed an extremely high fever that would not go away with medication. The doctor thought it was the flu and prescribed antibiotics, but she never seemed to get back to feeling well. Michelle became nauseated and cried much of the day. She just could not get comfortable and seemed to be in constant pain.

Within a few weeks Michelle was holding her head in a strange way—off to one side. Then she began walking with a stagger and finally began holding onto the wall for balance. Her vomiting became severe. Her mother and father, Barbara and Mike, were terribly frightened, but the doctor kept insisting it was just the flu. Still, they were convinced something was not right. They decided to seek a second opinion.

A CAT SCAN was immediately ordered. The family's fear turned into dreaded reality; the scan revealed that little Michelle had a tumor near her brain stem. She was diagnosed as having only months to live. She became her parents' little cross of nearly unbearable pain.

Two days later, Michelle was operated on to remove as much of the tumor as possible, and a biopsy later confirmed that she had a rare form of brain cancer. Aggressive chemotherapy was started, as the family prayed.

Several more brain surgeries were performed during the first two months of 1999, due to pressure on the brain caused by hydrocephalus. During that time, Michelle lost her eyesight for three weeks.

After being in the hospital for two months, Michelle and her mother, Barbara, came home—only to have to turn around and go back five days later. Complications from surgery and the side effects of chemotherapy had caused an infection of the lungs. She was rushed to intensive care and placed on life support.

The infection quickly worsened. Michelle became septic, and major organs began to fail, including the heart and kidneys. Doctors prepared the family for the worst. It seemed as if they had been in a traumatized state forever, but they doggedly bombarded heaven with prayers.

Michelle's mother was the leading prayer warrior for her "Little Cross," as she affectionately called her. Barbara had been given a rosary from Medjugorje by a friend who had been there on pilgrimage, and now she prayed the Rosary over and over.

During this time, Michelle was hardly ever alone. Although she was unable to open her eyes or move, her parents talked to her, touched her, and read to her. Friends came to be with her so that her exhausted mother could get a few hours sleep. Meanwhile her father, Mike, was home, doing his best to take care of their other two children and go to work each day.

One constant remained with all of the family members and friends as well: prayer. Prayers for the "Little Cross" were bringing the family even closer together. Her daily struggle for life served as inspiration to many who learned of her condition. Thousands of prayers were now being offered for the Little Cross.

Within days, things slowly began to turn around for Michelle. Eventually, the doctors were able to wean her off life support, and within thirty days she was out of intensive care and sent back to the oncology floor of the hospital. Her parents and family friends were convinced it was a miracle that she was still alive. They were sure the prayers had worked, but they remained realistic: More prayer would be needed.

After four more months of chemotherapy, Michelle's tumor had shrunk enough that the doctor was able to remove nearly all of it. That surgery was followed with more chemotherapy. Michelle began to get stronger and gradually went from not being able to even roll over by herself to sitting up unassisted and finally to standing with support. Mike and Barbara had high hopes that with therapy their little girl would eventually be able to walk again.

For nearly a year, Michelle seemed to be gaining in strength. But then a recurrence of the tumor sent her back into treatment in Houston, Texas, and away from her family for two and one-half months for radiation treatment. The doctors felt, given the choice, that this would be less risky than additional surgery. But while radiation stabilized the tumor, it failed to shrink it. Mike and Barbara again began a search for the best possible person to do the high-risk surgery.

A famous neurosurgeon in New York City was recommended, and in an operation in January 2000, eighty percent of the tumor was removed. Unfortunately, too much tumor remained to follow up with additional localized radio surgery, the next best option.

Since the surgery, Michelle had been kept relatively stable on chemotherapy until the fall of 2001, when symptoms indicated and diagnosis confirmed further growth of the tumor. The family's hopes for the continuation of life for little Michelle dimmed.

In January 2002 while in a Catholic bookstore, Barbara was drawn to my first book, *Medjugorje: The Message*. As she read the book, she told her husband, Mike, "Maybe Mary can help us."

Then in February, a friend invited Barbara to a Bible study, where she learned about an upcoming Marian conference. When she discovered that I was going to be the key speaker, she really wanted to go. During the conference, she passed by a table containing flyers about my upcoming Easter pilgrimage, not giving it much thought. The woman from her Bible study handed her a copy of the flyer and said, "You should go on this pilgrimage and take Michelle with you."

Barbara began thinking of all the reasons they could not go, but something inside her kept telling her she should. She then thought of Michelle's chemotherapy and thought it would be much too complicated to take her. But then she realized that because of a bout with pneumonia the month prior, Michelle's chemotherapy schedule had been rearranged such that she would be off treatment the two Fridays of the scheduled pilgrimage.

When Barbara's mother offered to financially help them and watch the other two other kids so that both Mike and Barbara could go with Michelle, the decision was made: They would be in Medjugorje for Easter and Holy Week. Hopes for a healing of the Little Cross were high.

❧

The pilgrimage to Medjugorje was phenomenal for Barbara and Mike—a trip they will never forget—and for all of us because of the presence of Michelle. She was immediately the "mascot" of the tour and a focal point for all of our prayers. We learned of her short life full of struggle and pain, and she became a special inspiration, displaying a constant smile. While the group was on Apparition Hill on Easter Sunday, during the time of the daily apparition, hands were laid on Michelle, prayers were said, and the experience was absolutely powerful and moving. Later during our trip Vicka also laid hands on Michelle, as did Father Jozo and a priest from the U.S. there on pilgrimage, Father Alan White.

I knew Father Alan from a previous pilgrimage to Medjugorje and immediately, upon seeing him in Colombo's Café, asked him to pray for Michelle and her family. Father Alan, who suffers from multiple sclerosis and has been blessed with the Holy Spirit gift of healing prayer, promised he would make this a top priority.

Weeks after the pilgrimage my thoughts and prayers were still centered on Michelle. Like Geraldine, and so many others I had met in the years of spreading the Medjugorje message, she became part of my daily prayers for a miracle healing. My prayers for these little warriors were always punctuated with the words "May your will be done." With so many people praying for Michelle, I looked for another miracle. It came, but not the way Michelle's parents, I, and others thought it would. The miracle was final peace for Michelle.

The Little Cross passed away two months later after years of non-ending medical treatment to save her life. It was a bittersweet moment for her family. Even in grief, they realized the grace of the special pilgrimage during Holy Week. Michelle had touched so many people. Her abbreviated mission in life was over, but her memory would last forever in the hearts and souls of all of us who shared and benefited from that experience with her.

Inexplicably, upon hearing of Michelle's passing, I immediately thought of Father Slavko's sudden death on Cross Mountain in November 2000. The followers of the apparitions were shocked and filled with grief as news of his passing spread. That grief turned into pure joy the next day when Our Lady gave her monthly message, ending it with this line: *"I rejoice with you and desire to tell you that your brother Slavko has been born into heaven and intercedes for you."*

The relationship of the life and death of little Michelle, Father Slavko, and Geraldine is this: Each served their life mission to completion and then passed on to eternal rest. For Father Slavko, it was fifty-two years; for Geraldine, twenty years; and, for Michelle, just five years.

Regardless of chronological age, each of us lives long enough to fulfill God's plan of salvation, individually and collectively. The Little Cross certainly fulfilled hers.

❦

"Dear children! Today I call you to open yourselves to prayer. May prayer become joy for you. Renew prayer in your families and form prayer groups. In this way, you will experience joy in prayer and togetherness. All those who pray and are members of prayer groups are open to God's will in their hearts and joyfully witness God's love. I am with you, I carry all of you in my heart and I bless you with my motherly blessing. Thank you for having responded to my call."

Monthly message given to the visionary Marija,
September 25, 2000.

TWENTY

The gift of fasting

On June 24, 1982, the Blessed Virgin Mary gave the visionaries this message: *"Thank the people in my name for the prayers, the sacrifices, and the penance. Have them persevere in prayer, fasting, and conversion and have them wait with patience for the realization of my promise. Everything is unfolding according to God's plan."*

Thus did the Blessed Virgin establish at Medjugorje the cornerstones of the Medjugorje messages: prayer, fasting, and penance. Of these, fasting is usually the most difficult to maintain, and inevitably the first to diminish or cease being an active part of the conversion process.

All of the cornerstones are gifts of the Holy Spirit and must be asked for with the heart of a believing child. Each supports and bonds into a strong base with the other.

Fasting is not an option if one is to live the Medjugorje message; it is requested of all—including the young. Our Lady gave a message on July 1982 that emphasizes this: *"The best fast is on bread and water. Through fasting and prayer, one can stop wars; one can suspend the laws of nature. Charity cannot replace fasting. Those who are not able to fast can sometime replace it with prayer, charity, and a confession; but everyone, except the sick, must fast."*

That is the thought process I try to convey to young people when speaking about fasting. I often compare the gift of fasting to the primitive drawings done with crayons that many parents receive from their children during the child's toddler years. For the child, it is the utmost expression of happy love; for the parents, each drawing becomes an art treasure to be displayed on the kitchen refrigerator door with magnets to serve as a constant reminder of the child's love. Soon the door is covered because the parents don't want to throw any of them away.

I tell youths that the gift of fasting is seen by God in very much the same way. Every fast, regardless of its value—whether it is a strict fast of bread and water, or a weak attempt that fails or only lasts a few hours—is a precious treasure to Him. It isn't the material value of the gift, but the sincere love and effort put forth. The value of the gift is dependent on the effort put forth.

How can young people—much less adults—practice the gift-giving of fasting in today's contemporary world when there is a fast food (no pun intended!) outlet on every corner? For most teenagers and many adults, fasting is nearly impossible. That is why Our Lady tells us to pray for the gifts. As she states emphatically in one of her messages listed above, with prayer and fasting we can stop wars and alter the laws of nature. It takes a concerted, focused effort of prayer and fasting to create miracles of the flesh and miracles of the soul.

Fasting, then, is allowing the spirit to overrule the flesh. The length of the fast is secondary to the effort put into it. But that does not take the humanity out of the attempt. I discovered this during an early stay at the visionary Marija's home.

I was having a casual conversion with a young woman named Kathleen, who stayed with Marija for more than three years serving as friend, traveling companion, and helper. She had been invited by Marija to fill this role on a spur-of-the-moment meeting. Kathleen humbly accepted without a second thought and dedicated the next three years of her life living with and helping Marija. I had met her during my first trip to Medjugorje in May 1986.

Kathleen and I had just finished a modest fast day evening meal of bread and plain soup. "You know," I said with a chuckle, "you get used to this fasting business after a while, but still, I really look forward to the next morning when I can freely eat anything I want again."

Kathleen smiled. "Yes, Marija and I are also like that."

I was surprised by her statement, thinking surely a visionary must fast with total dedication and no thoughts of ordinary things like being hungry. I continued: "What gets me is that a lot of young people I have met tell me that they sincerely try and fast on just bread and water, but that they get very hungry by nighttime; so then at midnight, they raid the refrigerator!"

Kathleen let out a loud laugh. "Oh, Marija and I do that all the time!"

I've never forgotten that conversion with Kathleen, and I repeat it constantly to young people who, like the little toddlers with the crayon drawings, are doing their best to give a good gift to God.

"Dear children, today I invite you to pray for peace. At this time, peace is threatened in a special way and I am seeking from you to renew fasting and prayer in your families. Dear children, I desire you to grasp the seriousness of the situation and that much of what will happen depends on your prayers; and you are praying a little bit. Dear children, I am with you and I am inviting you to begin to pray and fast seriously, as in the first days of my coming. Thank you for having responded to my call."

Monthly message given to the visionary Marija,
July 25, 1991.

TWENTY ONE

Sean: Tears on Our Lady's face

"I really liked your video," the visionary Mirjana told Sean. "I especially liked the way it ended. The whole time watching I felt the hairs on my arms standing up!"

Sean smiled and thanked her for the compliment. If anyone could give him confirmation that his new video *The Fruits of Mary* was good in the eyes of Our Lady, it would be the Medjugorje visionaries. Just hours earlier the visionary Ivan had also given him a "thumbs up" on the video.

It was the fourth trip for Sean Bloomfield to the village where the Virgin Mary had appeared daily for so many years. That in itself was a small miracle, said Sean, as he ruefully recalled his pre-Medjugorje days. He had returned this time to begin filming for his third documentary video, cementing a budding career in film journalism.

From a personal standpoint, it was hard for Sean to believe that several years earlier his life had been on a very different path. His change in direction had begun in 2001 when he realized his life was in ruins. He was twenty-one years old, still basking in the so-called "College Experience," drinking excessively and taking everything in life for granted. Religious faith was fuzzy—half believing, half not believing in a real God. Most of his Sundays were spent nursing hangovers. Easter was nothing more than a time for spring break and beach parties. Sean simply had no real direction spiritually or professionally.

Sean knew that education was the key to a good life, and that writing is what he wanted to do. After receiving a writing scholarship to attend the University of Tampa, he won an array of creative writing, screenwriting, and filmmaking awards. In those days, though, most of his creative output was replete with the cynicism and the common denial of Christian thinking that come when many young people begin developing intellectual and career skills.

Although a baptized Roman Catholic, Sean had not set foot in a church for over a decade. He disliked the thought of giving up part of a weekend for something about which he was unsure. He felt he believed in God, but years before, a group of young fundamentalist Christians, who shared lockers near his in high school, had turned him away from Christianity with their talk about how other religions were purely wrong or evil, and how Christ would never accept a non-Christian person.

Sean observed and listened as these so-called Christian peers disparaged and gossiped about fellow students like Ahmed, a gentle Muslim boy from Saudi Arabia, and little Jacob, a soft-spoken Jewish boy who proudly wore his Star of David on a necklace. They put down everyone who did not share their beliefs. These prejudiced comments, which Sean mistakenly took as representative of all Christians, gave him a sour taste for the whole of religion.

Although he could not fathom the events that lay ahead, the young man's jaded view of Christianity was about to change. His mother called him with a strange proposal: "Sean, will you come with me to Bosnia?"

"Sure," he had replied jokingly. "Let me pack my bags."

But Sean was surprised to find that she was serious. There was a trip going to Medjugorje in less than a week, and there were a few open spots. Only six months before, she had initially gone to Medjugorje on pilgrimage. Listening to his mother talk of her trip, despite his dismissal of Christianity, Sean found himself fascinated by her journey back to religion.

Barbara's Medjugorje calling had actually begun at a Florida antique store when she purchased several books, written in German, about the Third Reich and Nazi Germany. At the time, Barbara—twice divorced and looking for answers to life's questions—was immersed in the New Age movement. After a series of dreams and past-life regressions, she truly believed she had been reincarnated from the soul of a dead German man. Primarily, though, the books looked attractively old to her and would make good additions to her antique bookshelf.

The night Barbara took the books home, strange things started to happen. The first instance occurred while she was reading in her bedroom. She heard what sounded like the garbled voice of a child coming from the living room, followed by the sound of her dog, a female Labrador, growling and barking.

Barbara rushed out of her room to find the dog in the middle of the living room, its back bristling in fear, cowering and growling at nothing.

That night, Barbara lay asleep in her bed. She woke to the sound of her bedroom door creaking. No windows were open, and the dogs were in their pens. She finally went back to sleep, but repeatedly she would wake to the sound of the door creaking, and each time the door was cocked at a different angle.

During this ordeal, Sean's mother suffered from nightmares in which she dreamed that demonic beings were chasing her. Throughout the house she also continued to see strange images that would disappear or meld into shadow. And her television set kept turning on by itself, always tuned to a cartoon channel even though she never watched cartoons.

At the advice of her parents, Barbara finally called a local Catholic priest named Father Rick. He walked through the house, dispersing blessings and holy water. She told him about the events that had transpired.

"Has anyone died in this house?" Father Rick asked.

"No," Barbara replied. "It's a brand-new house, and I'm the first person to live here."

"Has anyone died recently in your family?"

"No, not for many years."

"Have you recently brought anything into the house?"

Barbara turned to the bookshelf and pointed. "I just bought those old books."

Father Rick approached the books cautiously and sprinkled them with holy water. "I don't even want to touch these," he said. "The books are the problem. Get them out of here immediately."

Barbara got rid of the books, and that was the last she heard of the restless spirit. But one thing remained: her new fascination with Catholicism. She had seen the power of Jesus in her own home. Father Rick invited her to visit Medjugorje on a pilgrimage group. Her first experience there brought her back into the Church, even to the point of becoming a Eucharistic minister.

Thus, when Sean's mother invited him to accompany her to Medjugorje on her second pilgrimage, he promptly agreed. "Why not—it's a free vacation!"

Within a week Sean was soaring high above the Atlantic. His seat was right beside Father Rick's. They talked for the entire flight. Unbeknownst to the young man, his conversion journey had begun.

From the time the plane approached the airport in Split, Croatia, Sean felt as if he was locked in a daydream. There was something surreal about the whole thing. Here he was, an American college kid, in a global region that modern media had labeled "The Powder Keg of the World."

Many times Sean had heard the strange story about what was supposedly happening in Medjugorje. As a journalist-in-training, he was skeptical of the story. Remembering the experiences of the so-called Christian kids in high school, he knew it would take nothing less than hard evidence to fully convince him that the happenings in Medjugorje were real.

❦

On his first afternoon in Medjugorje, Sean attended Mass in St. James Church with the rest of the group. As he listened to the priest, he tried to recall when he had last been to church, but could not remember. Sean had to watch what the other people were doing and then try and mirror their ways, so as not to look like an alien among them. His uneasiness was heightened when it was time for the Eucharist, and he had to remain at the pew while everyone else moved solemnly to receive Christ. Although a "cradle Catholic," he had never received First Communion because he had never taken Catechism classes.

Later, Sean sat alone in the churchyard and stared up at Cross Mountain as the sun sank low on the horizon, setting the hills ablaze. Had he made a mistake by coming here, he wondered? It didn't seem like he fit in with the crowd. Having been raised by a loving, yet unreligious father, he had virtually no concept of faith. He remained hard-set against organized religion because of his experiences with the claimed Christian classmates against those who were not Christians, and because he did not understand it.

Sean's place of "worship" had always been the wilderness, as a fishing guide and an outdoorsman. He had immersed himself in nature and had learned the basic values of patience and contemplation. He had never learned these values in a church pew being addressed by a priest. Thus, he decided to experience Medjugorje the way he knew best: He grabbed his backpack and headed for the outskirts of the little village, leaving a note at the pilgrim home where they were staying, telling his mother not to worry, that he had gone to climb Apparition Hill alone and would be back by sunrise.

But something strange was happening as Sean began making his way to Podbrdo. He felt he was being led, instead, to Cross Mountain, a much more difficult climb. For whatever reason, he changed direction and headed toward the mountain with the cross that protectively overshadows the village.

Sean walked through the narrow Medjugorje streets as children and old women stared at him from open windows. It felt good to be alone in such a foreign world, surrounded by the trappings of a different culture, he thought. A few chickens followed him until he got to the base of the mountain. An elderly woman had just ambled down the mountain, and Sean noticed that she was barefoot.

"Did you go all the way like that?" Sean asked her.

"Peccato," she said in Italian, smiling. And then, in English, she whispered, "for my sins."

Staring up at the far-off peak, the young naturalist removed his shoes and put them in his backpack. He had heard from the other pilgrims that climbing the mountain barefoot was a good way to be relinquished of the burdens of one's sins. Well, he thought, if an old woman could do it, then he would have to try.

The worn path was a painful combination of sharp, gray rocks and briar-laced vines. At different intervals along the climb, Sean stopped to pray at the large, bronze Stations of the Cross displays. He sincerely prayed that he might be granted some sort of sign that the Medjugorje phenomenon was real. At the same time, he took advantage of the time to rest his aching feet.

The sun had nearly set, and the mountain was bathed in pinkish light. Sean trudged along a straightaway in the trail. Up ahead he could see the third Station of the Cross display. As he had been doing for nearly the entire climb, he glanced down to watch his step, and then looked up again to be sure he was walking in the right direction. It was then that he saw a figure turning the corner just fifteen feet away, coming toward him.

The man was dressed in a white priest's robe, as if at the altar during Mass, and he had an enormous rosary around his neck. Sean glanced quickly again at his feet, making sure not to step in any precarious places. In this brief moment, he thought to himself, "What the heck is this priest doing on a mountain dressed like that?"

Sean looked up again for the strange man, but he was gone. He had vanished right in front of him! An overwhelming feeling of awe and wonder rushed through him as he ran to the spot where the man in the white robe had been standing just seconds before. He looked in the nearby briars to see if the man were playing some sick joke on him, but he was alone.

Sean's imagination began racing; could that have been—?

Beaming with happiness and an inexplicable inner understanding that something "holy" had just occurred, Sean dropped to his knees and thanked God.

The rest of his climb was under the darkness of night, and the stars overhead shone vividly. After nearly two hours of climbing, Sean finally rounded the last steep bend. Towering over him was the huge concrete cross. It stood so beautifully with the cosmos as a backdrop.

The very second Sean stepped on the pathway leading to the cross, a meteorite dashed across the sky, fizzling out behind the cross. Sean made his way to the altar and sat on the cool cement, dazedly but happily peering down at the lights of Medjugorje far below. Hesitantly, he took out a rosary that his mother had given him, along with a pamphlet that explained how to use it. After seeing the "priest" disappear earlier, he had promised himself that he would learn how to pray the Rosary. Using his flashlight to read, while clenching each tiny bead, he began reciting the prayers. The newly emerging convert prayed for his family and friends and even for those who had wronged him in the past.

During the next week in Medjugorje, Sean stayed mostly with the group, trying to spend time with his mother, Barbara, whom he hadn't actually lived with since he was five years old. One night, as he and his mother were sitting on the porch of the house, they noticed that the cross on Cross Mountain was glowing red. They could think of no explanation as to how it could have been glowing.

Toward the end of the pilgrimage, Sean and his group took a bus to Siroki Brijeg, to the church where Father Jozo Zovko was stationed. Inside the church, they listened to Father Jozo speak through an interpreter about his experiences with Our Lady. Sean thought he was the most peaceful-looking man he had ever seen. After he finished speaking, Father Jozo asked the priests in the audience to approach the altar. Father Rick went up with several others and knelt as Father Jozo prayed over them.

Sean was unsure of what was happening. The priests began to cry. Father Jozo then asked the entire audience to line up side by side along the inside walls of the church. Soon the priests began to pray over each of the pilgrims that were lined up. Sean was standing alongside his mother, and when he asked her what was happening, Barbara shushed him without giving an explanation.

Sean watched one of the priests praying over a man, and suddenly the man fell backwards with his eyes closed, into the waiting arms of two volunteers serving as "catchers". On the other side of the church, he watched as a woman collapsed as well. "What in the world is happening?" Sean thought to himself. He had seen things like this happen on late-night evangelical television shows, but had always laughed at what he thought was very poor acting. Surely these people were faking, or possibly they were overwhelmed with emotion.

But as he watched, Sean saw more and more people, some of them from his group, falling down as if asleep.

Soon Father Rick made his way to where Sean and Barbara were standing. He began to pray over Barbara, and Sean watched in disbelief as his mother went down. Father Rick came to stand in front of Sean, who suddenly sensed the two catchers behind him. Father Rick put his hands over Sean's forehead; it felt as if an electrical current was surging through his veins. His knees grew weak, and soon he could no longer feel his arms. The most pleasant warmth overtook him, but he fought it; he absolutely did not want to fall down, and he battled to regain his senses. It worked.

Father Rick moved to the young woman to Sean's left and began to pray over her. Sean was still reeling from what had just happened. A strange buzzing was going through his body, but at least he was not on the ground like the others. But then, catching him off guard, Father Rick suddenly put his other hand over Sean's head again, and peace swept over him like warm water. He began to go down!

Sean clenched onto some inner strength and again regained his senses and stood up before his body could touch the floor. Later, he regretted not allowing himself to be overtaken by whatever was pulsing through his body. Although he experienced that strange bliss for only a few seconds, Sean realized that the sinful life he had been living would do nothing to help him achieve that feeling again.

"Dear children! Today, again, I invite you to pray, so that through prayer, fasting, and small sacrifices you may prepare yourselves for the coming of Jesus. May this time, little children, be a time of grace for you. Use every moment and do good, for only in this way will you feel the birth of Jesus in your hearts. If with your life you give an example and become a sign of God's love, joy will prevail in the hearts of men. Thank you for having responded to my call."

Monthly message given to the visionary Marija,
November 25, 1996.

TWENTY TWO

Sean: Part II

Sean Bloomfield left Medjugorje so filled with peace that he was determined not only to change his life, but also to help spread the message. After graduating from college in May 2001, he decided to put his filmmaking skills to work by making a video about Medjugorje. It was by far the most effective way for him to spread the message. He went to work preparing for his production—which would not be easy, since he had no money.

The young entrepreneur needed more than three thousand dollars to buy the right video equipment. But as Our Lady had promised, "*One can stop wars and change the laws of nature through prayer and fasting.*" Sean began to seriously pray and fast.

His grandmother Mary had recently sold her business and felt compelled to help Sean purchase what he needed to begin his filmmaking business. Before he knew it, he was on his way to Medjugorje again. He would be there for the twentieth anniversary of the apparitions.

This time Sean would be staying with Jakov, the youngest visionary, in the small *pansion* attached to his house. Jakov's shyness was evident, but beneath it all, Sean could see wisdom far beyond his years. He agreed to let Sean interview him for the video, and one of his comments helped him see a more tolerant side of Christianity. "Our Lady is calling everyone to conversion, not just Catholics," Jakov told Sean. "The messages that Our Lady is giving here in Medjugorje are for the whole world, for all humanity. Our Lady always comes as a mother. She is a mother to all."

Sean heard about a possible miracle that was still occurring: The enormous bronze statue of the risen Christ, situated behind the church and the village cemetery, was exuding a strange liquid. After snaking through the crowd that had formed around the statue, he watched in amazement as water, or something resembling water, dripped from its left knee area. The liquid dripped non-stop for nearly a week, and he was there to record it.

Sean soon began to realize that his entire film shoot was blessed. Visionaries, priests, and pilgrims were open to on-camera interviews, and it seemed as if miracles were happening everywhere. By the end of the pilgrimage, he had more than enough material to produce a documentary video, which came to be called *Medjugorje in the New Millennium*.

Back home in Florida, the young filmmaker realized that his spiritual life had changed dramatically. He no longer cared about the sinful life he had once led. Peace was all he sought. Prayer had become part of his daily routine, a new kind of praying that had previously been foreign—prayer from the heart, as Jakov had described it. He worked hard to follow the messages of Medjugorje.

Things in his life were moving at a dizzying pace. Sean now saw a lot of things differently, including plans for marrying and having a family. He proposed to his longtime girlfriend, Lisa, with a simple prayer: "God, please let her say yes!"

After the successful release of his first documentary video, Sean knew he could do more to help spread the messages. He wanted to make a documentary that compared Medjugorje with other Marian apparition sites. Things progressed in rapid succession: He traveled to Lourdes, Garabandal, and Fatima, and was even marooned in Fatima during the September 11, 2001, terrorist attack tragedies.

Sean was soon invited back to Medjugorje to stay with the visionary Ivan, who allowed Sean to film him during apparitions and granted him several interviews. "Conversion does not happen overnight," Ivan told him during an interview. "It is a lifelong process. Conversion starts with peace."

During this pilgrimage, Sean fulfilled what he felt was a milestone in his conversion: He officially joined the Catholic Church. It started by giving a general confession to a young priest. When it was over, he had never felt so free. Soon afterward, Sean Bloomfield finally received his First Communion.

The remainder of the newest video came together through strange coincidences. On his flight home, Sean was seated next to a U. S. State Department worker who had lived in Bosnia during the war. Her photos of the devastation came to be featured in the video. Upon returning home, Sean came into contact with a Hollywood special effects animator named Brian DeMetz. It turned out that Brian was a strong believer and promoter of Medjugorje. He created some amazing special effects for the video. When it was finally released, *The Fruits of Mary* was very well received. Sean soon began thinking of a third video.

And so Sean returned to Medjugorje for a fourth visit in May 2004, this time staying with the visionary Mirjana, and accompanied by a group that included his fiancée, Lisa.

After speaking with Sean about *The Fruits of Mary*, Mirjana sat down for an on-camera interview with him. "The Blessed Mother comes to me so that we may pray together for unbelievers," Mirjana told him. "She doesn't call them unbelievers, but rather 'those who have not yet felt the love of God.' Those of us who already believe can change them, but only with our prayers and with our example."

This particular statement hit Sean hard. Lisa had been raised with no religious background, yet she was the nicest, most honest person Sean had ever known. Still, it was difficult for him to live his new faith with her as an outsider. He truly wanted Lisa to witness the benefits of religion, and following the interview with Mirjana, Sean prayed that Lisa might see the light. That evening, she literally did.

The young couple went to one of Ivan's nighttime apparitions at the base of Apparition Hill. When the apparition was about to begin, Lisa found herself standing on a rock outcropping just beside where Ivan was kneeling. While the people around her bowed their heads in prayer, Lisa studied the scene and saw a strange ball of light glide overhead and disappear into the brush on the hillside. She soon saw the light again, and this time it was coming down the hillside toward the crowd. Just as the light approached Ivan, it pulsed brightly three times before vanishing, and then Ivan went into ecstasy. This experience helped make Lisa a believer.

"It's so sad when Blessed Mary is talking about unbelievers," Mirjana told Sean as they were completing the last of the interviews. "Sometimes I see tears on Our Lady's face because of them. We are all her children, believers and unbelievers. Praying for the unbelievers is like cleaning the tears from Our Lady's face."

Clearly, Sean's conversion and ongoing spreading of the messages through his filmmaking has helped clean the tears from Our Lady's face.

"Dear children! Also today I call you to pray from your whole heart and to love each other. Little children, you are chosen to witness peace and joy. If there is no peace, pray and you will receive it. Through you and your prayer, little children, peace will begin to flow through the world. That is why, little children, pray, pray, pray, because prayer works miracles in human hearts and in the world. I am with you and I thank God for each of you who has accepted and lives prayer with seriousness. Thank you for having responded to my call."

Monthly message given to the visionary Marija,
October 25, 2001.

TWENTY THREE

The darkest sin

I truly believe the worst sin of our times is abortion. I believe this because it is the greatest destroyer of young life. The destruction is not only within the womb but in the heart, mind, and soul of the victim mothers, as well as the young men involved. I know this firsthand, because my daughter Lisa had an abortion and we, as a family, went through its trauma.

The decision young people are faced with as a consequence of their actions, to accept or give up a precious new life in the womb, is heavily influenced by contemporary mores. The mantra sung to the victim mothers-to-be by misguided individuals, liberal politicians, secular organizations driven by self-serving concerns for women, and the general media is this: It is your body, your choice, your right. It is a mantra of secularism and humanism without a thought of morality and spirituality.

Even though my family was directly affected by the sin of abortion, the emphasis on speaking out on the sin of abortion did not come into sharp focus for my mission until May 1989. It was during a unique weekend in which Pentecost Sunday and Mother's Day would be celebrated on the same day. I would be speaking at two separate conferences that weekend; the first would be Saturday morning at a small conference in Virginia Beach, Virginia, and the second would be Saturday evening at a much larger one at Notre Dame University.

On Friday evening before the start of the Virginia Beach conference, I sat with the other invited speakers and some of the early attendees for an informal chat. From the beginning of that conversation, abortion was the dominant topic. The formal meeting lasted more than two hours. During the entire evening, I thought of my daughter Lisa, but I hesitated to bring such a personal matter into our discussion. Still, I went to bed deeply affected by the passion of our discussion and its relationship to what Lisa had been through.

The next afternoon, I flew to Notre Dame in South Bend, Indiana, with the thoughts of the previous evening still dancing in my mind.

The time at the Notre Dame conference was a blur. I again honed in on the sin of abortion during my brief twenty-minute talk. I spoke of Our Lady's telling us that with prayer we could stop wars and alter the laws of nature, and stated that abortion was the most critical war of all. I also emphasized that it tied in perfectly with Mother's Day and the gift of healing given us by the Holy Spirit. Yet again, I held back from mentioning Lisa's experiences; this was something that she would have to agree to before I could do it.

However, it was in the early morning of that special Sunday that all the talk and thought on the subject of the sin of abortion came together from that compact twenty-four hours.

I was half-dozing in the early morning hours, anticipating the private Mother's Day and Pentecost Sunday Mass at a small chapel on the Notre Dame campus. I suddenly had a powerful twilight dream, bathed in brilliant light and clear as any vision in content and meaning: A delicate woman's hand—I instantly knew it was the Blessed Virgin Mary's hand—came toward me holding a tiny, lucent hand. It was the hand of an unborn fetus.

The meaning of the dream or vision was clear: Making people aware of the horrible sin of abortion was to be a permanent part of my Medjugorje mission from that moment on. I could hardly wait for the next opportunity.

❦

That opportunity came several days later as I arrived in California for an extended tour of speaking engagements in churches in and around Los Angeles and along the southern end of the West Coast. I launched into a blunt, strong attack on the evils of abortion and its relationship to Our Lady's messages at Medjugorje. "She is urging, pleading, and begging us to pray, fast, and do penance to bring an end to this slaughter of the innocents," I practically shouted to the audience.

Immediately, there began a slow but steady exodus of listeners, mainly women. It continued throughout the talk, and by the end, over one-third of the audience had left, with many casting scowling, angry glances my way as they exited.

I stayed at the front of the church, answering questions and talking to people, and received many encouraging comments about continuing to talk about the evil of abortion as it related to the Medjugorje messages. Still, I was upset that so many people had left. I had never experienced that before.

One young lady stood to one side, nervously waiting for the others to leave so that she could speak to me. Several times I thought she might bolt, but she stayed until everyone else had left before timidly approaching me.

As I took her hand, the young lady began softly crying, looking down at the floor. "What can I do to help you?" I asked, gently lifting her chin so that I could see her face.

It took a few moments before she could answer. "I just wanted to ask you a question," she whispered, as she glanced from side to side to make sure no one was within hearing distance. There were more tears, and she looked at me with great distress before asking: "Do you think God will forgive me for having an abortion?"

Suddenly, my concern for the exodus of attendees no longer mattered. If nothing else, one young woman had been touched by the talk, and that was all that mattered at that moment. I also thought of the years of agony my own daughter had suffered from the guilt of her actions. "Yes," I said to her, smiling, "a thousand times yes!" I then suggested that she find a priest and confess and then do the best she could at living the life God intended for her.

The young lady looked as if the world had just been lifted from her shoulders. She quickly hugged me while whispering "thank you" over and over, and then hurried out of the church.

I knew right then that I would never again hesitate to speak out on the darkest sin of our time. I also knew I needed to have a similar conversation with Lisa.

"Dear children! Today I call you to have your life be connected with God the Creator, because only in this way will your life have meaning and you will comprehend that God is love. God sends me to you out of love, that I may help you to comprehend that without Him there is no future or joy and, above all, there is no eternal salvation. Little children, I call you to leave sin and to accept prayer at all times, that you may in prayer come to know the meaning of your life. God gives Himself to him who seeks Him. Thank you for having responded to my call."

Monthly message given to the visionary Marija,
April 25, 1997.

TWENTY FOUR
Lisa: Witness for life

"You can do it, Lisa."

"No, Daddy, I can't—not yet. I'm just not ready; it's too hard."

Tears rolled down my daughter's cheeks, and mental pain masked her face. We sat in the speaker's lounge of the Irvine, California, Medjugorje Conference just before she was scheduled to speak. More than 6,000 people were in attendance. It was the first time that we both had been invited to speak at the same conference. I was asking her once again to witness about her abortion. It was a familiar conversation with the same result.

Adding to the drama, this particular conference was an outcropping of the original tour of California during which I first began speaking out about the sin of abortion, and was now in its fourth year. I felt in my heart it was the perfect place and time for Lisa to finally do what I knew she had to do. But it would have to be her decision. I sighed as I put my arms around my oldest child. "Okay, kid. Just pray to the Holy Spirit and what comes, comes." I let it go at that.

Composing herself, Lisa promised that one day she would tell the world about having had an abortion, but not just yet. I believed her because Our Lady had put it in my heart that my "*family would be involved in spreading the messages . . .*" and Lisa, more than any other member of the family, was the fulfillment of that prophecy. Our Lady had also revealed that my daughter, because of the abortion, would never have children. That was a tremendous cross she carried in the silence of her heart.

Sitting in the front row of the huge auditorium crammed with people, I thought about the events that had led to Lisa's suffering. It began as a result of another great sin of our time—divorce.

As a twelve-year-old, Lisa had experienced the crisis of a child of a broken marriage. She was old enough to understand fully that her family was being destroyed. The constant tugging for support from both parents, as well as having to be the big sister and cope with the needs and fears of her brothers and sister, had developed in her a sense of bitterness and insecurity that soon turned to hard cynicism.

After graduating from college in 1983 and obtaining a good job, Lisa was determined to live the good life to fill the emptiness of lost family love; she was open to anything that might make up for it.

Blessed with good looks and a pleasant personality, Lisa was popular and loved to have a good time. She had more than her share of it during and after college, finally settling into an all-too-intimate relationship with a young man named David whom she had met at school.

One day in May of 1985, the cold reality of her lifestyle hit without warning: Lisa discovered she was pregnant.

My daughter was shocked. She was on birth control pills and savvy enough to know and use the easily available contemporary measures of modern-day relationships between young people. An out-of-wedlock pregnancy was the last thing she expected to happen to her.

Life at the time was looking pretty good. Lisa had a great job, wore fashionable clothes, and knew how to live in the material world. David was a nice enough young man, but without a lot of ambition. The pregnancy threatened to ruin everything.

Frightened and ashamed, my cosmopolitan daughter, suddenly a desperate little girl again, called and tearfully gave me the grim news. I was glad that despite the soap-opera turmoil of ongoing family trials caused by the divorce, we had become close as father and daughter. More important, we were friends.

I went to her immediately, my mind racing during the long drive to her apartment in Columbia. What should I say or do to help her? She hadn't told her mother and didn't plan to. She just couldn't, she tearfully told me as we sat in her apartment tightly gripping hands. The doctors had said the chances were good that she would miscarry due to medical problems they had discovered during the examination, and that . . . she should have an abortion.

Even though my own spiritual life at this time was at best lukewarm (this was months before I learned about the apparitions at Medjugorje), I knew abortion was morally wrong. I tried to talk her out of it and urged her to go ahead and have the child, and added that I would help her and support her.

But Lisa had made up her mind to go through with the abortion, rationalizing that based on the doctor's opinion she might lose the baby anyway. I was devastated.

The unspoken truth was, to give birth to a baby as a single mother at this particular time would totally disrupt Lisa's lifestyle—and bring with it a shame she could never live down.

Lisa had the abortion and began the struggle to return to a normal life. Less than a year later, she further complicated her struggles by accepting David's proposal of marriage, and they were wed in March 1986. This was her way of trying to cover up one mistake with another.

Meanwhile, Medjugorje had come into my life in the throes of my daughter's struggles. Two months after her wedding, I was on my way to Medjugorje for my first pilgrimage. I came home on fire, and the first order of business was to convert my children—with Lisa topping the list.

I was met with total rejection. None of my children wanted to hear about Medjugorje—especially Lisa. Any thoughts of religion only made the inner agony of having had an abortion worse.

I literally cornered the kids when we were gathered together for any family function and began preaching to them. It took a while to realize that I needed to be quiet and just let them see what Medjugorje was doing for me and through me. Only then did the breakthrough with Lisa finally arrive.

Lisa had heard I was going to be speaking in Spartanburg, South Carolina, only a two-hour drive from her home in Columbia. She and her sister Angela had decided they would come and listen; what did I think of that?

"Great," I answered, trying not to let the surge of emotion show in my voice. "It will give us time to catch up on things."

I felt a warmth and a tingling sensation. Finally, Lisa was going to hear about the wonders of Medjugorje. I thanked God for this opportunity to possibly reach my daughters with the message, even though I was fully aware they were coming only to appease me.

Lisa had settled into marriage with David, and for the moment everything seemed to be fine. Yet, every time I saw her, even for the briefest of moments, her eyes reflected the anguish of knowing what she had done.

I drove to Spartanburg filled with all kinds of thoughts. Would this finally be the turning point? Was my firstborn at last coming to grips with the never ending pangs of guilt from having had an abortion? Would it help her sister, Angie, as well? She was in a troubled marriage and could also use a little spiritual boost. There were so many questions and doubts to dull my optimism.

The auditorium in Spartanburg was filled to overflowing; it was a good mix of Catholics and Protestants, as this northern South Carolina city was located in the heart of the "Bible Belt." My thoughts, however, were more focused on my daughters, Lisa in particular.

I didn't see Lisa and Angela until the talk began, wryly noting they had arrived at the last moment and had taken seats in the rear of the auditorium. This seemed to confirm my apprehensions that they had come only out of family obligation. Then as usual, everything but the message was blocked out. No longer was I thinking about them—or about the denominations of those present.

Afterward, people came to the front of the auditorium thanking me and asking questions. There were comments and inquiries from Protestants, one wanting to debate, quoting Scripture and asking for biblical proof of apparitions. I explained to him as best I could, but my mind was really on my daughters.

As the man left, the crowd began to thin. I glanced around furtively, looking for Lisa and Angela. Out of the corner of my eye, I spotted my daughters, still in the rear of the auditorium. Lisa was crying on Angela's shoulder. Angela caught my eye, shrugged, and turned her free hand up in an expression indicating that she didn't have a clue as to what was wrong with her older sister.

But I knew what was wrong with Lisa. This was the beginning of what would make everything right for her: She had been struck by the message.

It took a while to make my way through the crowd. Lisa had stopped crying until she saw me. A few moments later, with her arms wrapped tightly around my neck, she whispered softly, "Daddy, that wasn't you speaking. That was God, and He was talking to me. I really believe that, and . . . I want to go to Medjugorje!"

Now I had to fight back tears. After months of anguish, attempting to convince my daughter that this was the only solution to erase the sin of abortion from her soul, the conviction came to her in a matter of minutes. I recalled the beautiful words Our Lady had given me: "*. . . your family shall be united with you in the work you are to do. . . .*"

I left Spartanburg convinced the prophecy was coming true, and that Lisa would go to Medjugorje, be totally healed spiritually, and would tell the world about it. But it didn't work that way.

Lisa's healing from the sin of abortion did begin, but there would be other crosses along the way. I arranged for Lisa and my mother to go to Medjugorje on pilgrimage together in September 1988.

My daughter came home transformed. Soon she was quietly attending the Catholic Church and was deep into finding the joys of true belief. But this was having an adverse effect on her marriage to David. He wanted nothing to do with religion, especially Catholicism, since he was a Protestant at least in name. Within the year, he left Lisa.

Shortly after the separation, I took Lisa to a Medjugorje conference in New Orleans on the first weekend of December. I was one of the speakers at the conference, as was the

Medjugorje visionary Ivan. Lisa's birthday was December 2, the final day of the conference, and a special birthday present was that we would be present for Ivan's evening apparition at the home of local followers of the apparitions.

As we left the private home and prepared to return to our hotel, Lisa was filled with emotion, bringing a glistening to her eyes as she tried to contain herself. "Wow," I exclaimed as we waited for the car to take us to the hotel, "that was some birthday gift, huh?"

Lisa smiled wanly. "It was incredible," she said, and then finally she could no longer contain the tears. "Daddy, I just want to marry a good Catholic boy."

I promised my daughter on the spot that I would pray for that intention beginning immediately. When she returned home, she enrolled in Right of Christian Initiation for Adults classes.

Six months later, Lisa was actively involved in the Catholic Church. She was confirmed in April 1992, and two months later was working with the Catholic Youth Ministry. She had found her niche. It was there also she met a young man named Tom Militello who was also working as a youth leader. The two were soon good friends—and then, engaged. Two years later, with Lisa having obtained an annulment, they were married. Lisa had found her "good Catholic boy."

I was jarred back to the present as Lisa was being introduced. She stood at the podium for a few moments and then began speaking in a quavering voice. As she began, I realized that at last, Lisa was going to witness about her abortion. I had instant inner feelings of intense empathy and joy clashing with one another.

From the beginning, Lisa's telling her story took its toll. On both of us. I felt as though something was ripped from my stomach, but I was so proud of her. Lisa cried openly and at times had to pause to gain control. She left nothing out. The audience of 6,000 people was silently entranced, with the exception of stifled sobs as several young women left at intervals of her testimony.

My oldest daughter would continue her personal witness on the evils of abortion in our society. Soon she was being invited to many gatherings and had to begin delicately balancing an active speaking agenda with family life.

❦

As she has stressed so often in her messages at Medjugorje, the Blessed Virgin Mary is a willing intercessor for our needs. She constantly asks us, urges us, and pleads with us to put prayer in the first place in our lives to solve our personal and family problems. When we adhere to her formula of prayer and fasting, when we openly, confidently trust in heaven's grace, we are rewarded in like manner. The point was made in a tremendous way by Lisa's surrender to the will of the Holy Spirit.

I received a telephone call from my daughter late one Friday evening. "Tom and I thought we might come and see you guys this weekend if it's all right with you," she said. Then, after a slight pause, she added, "we have something wonderful to tell you."

"Sure, of course, come down," I answered, a little more than curious but not pushing for her to explain on the telephone.

Hardly had Lisa and Tom entered the house when, after exchanging greetings, she excitedly said, "Dad, you remember you told me you felt the Blessed Mother put it in your heart that I would never have children because of the abortion? Well," she beamed, putting her arm around Tom's waist, "we're pregnant!"

I was stunned. Then, I felt Our Lady speaking to my heart: *"This is a grace I have obtained for her. . . ."*

I immediately relayed the message to Tom and Lisa. We all just stood there hugging each other in silence—and the inevitable tears of joy flowed.

Today, Lisa and Tom are the proud, loving parents of three children. Meghan is now nine years old; her brothers Nick and Sam are six and two.

Lisa balances a rigorous, ongoing daily itinerary. She is above all a wife and a mother. She and Tom are still youth leaders at their church, and she is working for the South Carolina legislature on a part-time basis.

Somehow in the midst of it all, Lisa makes time to continue her public speaking mission to youths and young adults, telling her story over and over—and always to the painful accompaniment of tears.

In all aspects, my daughter is a beautiful witness to life.

"Dear children! With this message I call you anew to pray for peace. Particularly now when peace is in crisis, you be those pray and bear witness to peace. Little children, be peace in this peaceless world. Thank you for having responded to my call."

Message given to the visionary Marija,
on January 25, 2003.

TWENTY FIVE

Signs and wonders

A frequent supernatural sign seen at or through related events concerning Medjugorje is the phenomenon of rosary chains turning from a silver color to a gold color. Thousands of people have also witnessed the miracle of the sun seemingly spinning and dancing in the sky, sometimes surrounded by special symbols during its impossible movements. There have been healings, sightings reportedly of Our Lady at a distance, and other supernatural signs and wonders. The purpose of all of them is singular: to bring souls to spiritual conversion.

For many followers of Medjugorje, such signs and wonders launch them on a continuing path of conversion. But for some, it doesn't initially take hold, and it may be years later before the person realizes the grace given and recognizes and acts upon it. The following two stories illustrate this:

The packed audience sat enraptured as the teenage boy began giving his testimony. Young John had been asked by Father Slavko to speak from the altar at St. James Church in Medjugorje following the homily at the English-language mid-morning Mass. It was a special grace and honor for anyone other than a priest to speak from the altar, but especially so for a teenage boy from the United States.

I listened intently, sitting close to the front with a clear view of the young man as he related his testimony. How amazing it was to see and hear him witnessing in an unassuming, yet animated manner. As has been stated several times to this point, there is something uniquely powerful about spiritual witness from young people.

"The last thing I expected when I went out that night was to get arrested," John stated. "I never once stopped to think of the change that this one night would have on my life. . . ."

After his arrest for a minor violation, John found himself lost, sitting in a jail cell awaiting his parents' hoped-for rescue. The time in the cell, swathed in fear, triggered in him a heretofore-unexplored desire to find out just who he really was. What was it that led to his being here? What did he want to do with his life? Who was he and who was he destined to be?

After the "rescue," his parents began to think of what would be a suitable punishment for what their son had done. After two days John's father thought of a punishment that in John's mind far exceeded the definition of a "normal punishment." His idea was that John would be grounded until he finished reading the entire Bible.

As any kid would, John thought that the punishment was ridiculous. He fought his grounding for months, adamantly refusing to read the Bible. Finally, John's dad gave a little ground with a compromise: He decided that if John stopped arguing and constantly bothering him about the grounding, he would lower the requirement to reading only the New Testament.

John figured that this was better than nothing and told his dad that it was definitely something he could handle. That evening, he at last began, and opened the "big black book." Once again, he did not know how much *this* night would change his life.

John began flipping through the pages until he came upon the first Gospel of the New Testament, Matthew. He actually read completely through it but noticed that he had much left to read to complete the entire New Testament. He decided that instead of reading page for page he would skim through the rest and only retain the bare essential information that he needed to pass his dad's quiz when the assignment was completed.

To his surprise, John got through the New Testament in about two weeks, and although he had retained a great deal of what he had read, there was still much he had skipped. But he passed his dad's test.

Then something strange happened. Now free to be with his friends again, John decided on his own, not long after he was let off grounding, to start reading the Bible again—including the Old Testament. This time he would read every bit of it. In the process, young John discovered something very important about himself. He really did want to be good.

"I'm not quite sure of where I'm going with this from here," he said as he ended his witness in St. James Church, "but I know for sure that my life has changed for the better and that I'm happy about that."

Afterward, I made my way to the front of the church where the young speaker was surrounded by well-wishers. I introduced myself, and then, based on that now-familiar inner urging, I took his hand and poured my rosary beads into it. "I feel the Blessed Virgin wants me to give them to you." With that, I turned and left the church, leaving the young man looking a bit perplexed.

That afternoon, as I was giving a talk in one of the large tents behind the church, I noticed that John was in attendance. I didn't see him again for several days and was surprised one day when he and a priest who was with his group came to the home where I was staying. "Our group is leaving tomorrow," he told me, "but I wanted to see you before we left, so I hope I'm not bothering you."

I smiled at him. "Of course not. It's good to see you again."

John then told me that when I approached him in the church and gave him my rosary, he did not know that I had written books on Medjugorje. "I didn't know who you were when you gave me the rosary, but I found out when I came to your talk," he told me. "After the talk I went out and bought one of your books at a store here and I read it all." He then pulled out the rosary I had given him. "Thanks again for this; now I know how special it is."

I looked at the rosary and smiled. "John, look at the rosary."

John held the rosary up and looked at it. "Yeah, it's great. Thanks again."

I realized he hadn't noticed the change. "John, it's turned gold-colored since I gave it to you."

John and the priest stood there for a few moments in pure astonishment. And then, finally, in unison they emitted a long, low, "*Wow!*"

A few months later, I received from John via e-mail his full conversion story and how it was continuing to affect his daily life. Once again the signs and wonders of Medjugorje had touched a young soul.

❦

Many young people like John are easily moved by the signs and wonders stemming from the apparitions of Our Lady at Medjugorje. For the most part, John's case being an example, that is a good thing. However, some cases are like the parable of the seed in Holy Scripture where some seeds fall into shallow soil and sprout for a limited period before withering.

The same thing happens with those moved only by the sensationalism of the signs. The hope is that even if the sprouting withers, the roots of the seed remain and sprout again some day—stronger than before.

Five years ago in Medjugorje during the Youth Festival, I sat with a father and his teenage daughter on a bench outside the church as the evening service began with the praying of the Rosary. I had joined them purposely, sensing on first meeting them, the father's desire in bringing his daughter to Medjugorje and her resistance to being there.

Kevin McMahan, a retired policeman who had served twenty-eight years on the streets of New York City, was praying that his thirteen-year-old daughter Ann Marie would find a spark of faith through the Blessed Virgin Mary, whom he so dearly loved. Having gone through the heartbreak of divorce, he had spent far too little personal time with his daughter due to his workaholic approach to police work.

This was their first ever trip together, and Kevin had brought Ann Marie to this place of miracles with one thought in mind: her spiritual conversion. So far, she had responded little and seemed bored and out of place.

As I approached them on the bench, I noticed Kevin fervently praying and Ann Marie looking off into the distance and not participating in the prayers. "Mind if I join you?" I asked.

"Oh, sure, we'd be honored." Kevin moved over to make room for me.

As I took my place I asked Ann Marie, "So, what do you think of this place?"

Ann Marie glanced furtively at me and replied quietly, "It's okay."

But the look on her face said otherwise. She was noticeably not happy, still tired from the travel of getting there, and not sure why she had agreed to come here with her father in the first place. I let it go at that, joining in with her father in the Rosary prayers.

As we prayed, I did a double take as I noticed something happening to Kevin's rosary: It was changing from silver to gold as each bead was being prayed!

Kevin noticed nothing, having shut his eyes again to concentrate on the words of the prayers. Ann Marie continued staring out in space, not participating in the prayers. I smiled to myself and decided to say nothing at the time.

Upon completion of the prayers, I waited momentarily to see if Kevin would notice the difference in his rosary. He didn't. Instead, he asked me, "How many kids do you think are here this year?"

I ignored his question. "Kevin, Ann Marie, look at what has happened to your dad's rosary."

Kevin looked and then shook his head. "What do you mean?"

"Your rosary—look at it."

"Yeah, okay, what about it?" He still hadn't noticed, nor had Ann Marie.

"Kevin, your rosary has turned gold. I watched it turn as we prayed."

With that, Ann Marie now did a double take. Suddenly animated, she reached her hand out. "Dad, can I see it? Can I hold it?"

"Oh, my gosh, you're right," Kevin exclaimed, as he slowly handed the rosary to his daughter. "I can't believe that! What does it mean? That's incredible!"

I laughed, delighted, knowing that this was Our Lady at work again for one of her little souls. "Well," I began, "I think it means 'thank you' to you, Kevin, for praying her special

Rosary prayer, and to you, Ann Marie, it's to let you know that she is here for you."

I personally saw this little miracle of the rosary turning gold as a sign that another young soul would take the path to conversion. But I was mistaken; I would learn from Kevin later that the seed of faith took root briefly in his daughter, but in due time it had withered.

I discovered just how much it had withered in May 2005, when I went to Newark, New Jersey, for a week of talks at the initial invitation of Kevin. He had now been to Medjugorje with my tours four more times and had asked me several times to come to his home area and give talks. Tom Hyer, a gentleman from the same area who had also come on the November 2004 tour, had worked with Kevin to arrange five nights of talks in the region.

On the second night of the tour, I met with Ann Marie just before the time of the talk. She was now eighteen years old and had assembled a long history of personal problems. She seemed headed for a life of dark misery. Yet she had readily agreed to meet and talk with me.

We talked quietly in the secluded "cry room" (an enclosed room where mothers with small children can attend Mass) of the church where I would be giving my talk that evening. Ann Marie was a beautiful young woman, but lacked self-esteem and motivation to stay away from the elements that continued to create problems in her life. The very fact that she wanted to meet with me gave renewed optimism to her father.

I began asking questions. "Ann Marie, do you ever think back about the things that happened on your trip to Medjugorje?"

A quiet but blunt answer: "No, not really."

"But you do remember the rosary turning gold."

"Oh, yeah, that was neat."

"Where are you in your faith?"

With the last question, Ann Marie opened up slightly. She did believe in God and really wanted to do the right things. She realized she had messed up her life. At one point, she had gained too much weight, causing her greater unhappiness and low self-esteem.

However, like John in the previous story, Ann Marie had discovered something about herself. She had confronted her weight gain problem with a solution: She began walking long distances daily, and soon the weight was gone. The walking exercise has become a part of her daily routine, and she knows now that she can change other things in her life.

Ann Marie then said something that would give further hope to her father that his daughter would find that elusive spark of faith. Without prompting from me, Ann Marie said, "You know, I'd like to go back to Medjugorje with my father."

That one statement indicated that the root was still alive; there was hope that it might one day take hold and grow into a fruit producing a hundredfold yield.

That, of course, is the reason for the signs and wonders at Medjugorje.

"Dear children! Also today I call you to prayer. Little children, pray until prayer becomes a joy for you. Only in this way each of you will discover peace in the heart and your soul will be content. You will feel the need to witness to others the love that you feel in your heart and life. I am with you and intercede before God for all of you. Thank you for having responded to my call."

Monthly message given to the visionary Marija,
July 25, 2003.

TWENTY SIX

Milka: Why not me?

On the second day of the apparitions at Medjugorje—the day when conversation with the Blessed Virgin Mary actually began—six children from the village knelt before the beautiful woman in the light. They would become the Medjugorje visionaries who would bear her messages to the world. And they would soon be famous in their own right for having been so chosen.

One young girl who had seen Gospa on the first day was not present among the chosen six; instead, her sister Marija was there in her place. This would create resentments and haunt her for years to come.

Milka Pavlovic was tending to her mother's sheep near the base of Podbrdo Hill when the Blessed Virgin first appeared. The thirteen-year-old stood transfixed with a small knot of children, staring at the woman in the light who beckoned for them to come where she was. None of them went to her because of a mixture of fear and awe. But there was no doubt in the minds of the children that they were seeing the Blessed Virgin Mary. Milka, like the others, excitedly raced home to tell family and friends that she had seen Gospa.

Milka's story was met with admonishment by her mother. What was wrong with her, telling such tales? A day working in the fields alongside her mother would teach her not to tell such tales about Gospa.

And that is where the youngest sister of Marija was on that second day when she, like the others, felt an inner urge to return to the base of Podbrdo Hill at exactly the same time and place as the day before.

This time when the beautiful lady appeared, the children went to her. Marija was among them along with ten-year-old Jakov, a distant cousin. He had been at the Pavlovic home when the other children had come by to get Milka just before the time of the apparition. Since Milka was in a distant field working with her mother, they had urged Marija and Jakov to come with them in her place. Thus were the six visionaries assembled, and thus began the supernatural conversations that continue as of this writing.

Upon learning of Marija's inclusion on this second day of Gospa's appearance, Milka was extremely upset—and angry at her mother. Don't worry, her sister comforted her, come with me tomorrow and maybe you will also see her again.

On the third day of apparitions, Marija took Milka with her. "Here, stand behind me and pray that she appears to you, too," she told her sister. But when the apparition ended, Milka sadly related to her sister that she had not seen anything. She knew she would never see Gospa again as she had on that first day.

❧

From the moment I met Milka, I knew there was something special about her. It was more than just the story I had read of her having "been blessed" to see the Blessed Virgin Mary on the first day of the apparitions—and seemingly cursed to have been excluded as one of the six regular visionaries. I immediately noted in her a fierce independence and a confidence that made her fully capable of taking care of herself.

Sitting with friends at a small café, one of only a couple in all of Medjugorje at that time, Milka approached us to take our order. She was working as a waitress for her brother Antonio, who owned the café. Within minutes we were laughing and joking, she in the limited English she had picked up from the many English-speaking pilgrims now filling the village weekly. Before leaving the café, I asked her if she would agree to an interview with me, explaining that I was a journalist working on a book about Medjugorje.

"Why you want to interview me?" she answered with an easy smile. "I no visionary. Maybe you speak to my sister Marija."

"No," I responded resolutely, "it's you I want to interview, because I still consider you a visionary even though you only saw her that first day." I was especially interested in her acceptance of not being included as a regular visionary. After some more discussion, the interview was arranged.

From the interview and other meetings with Milka, she soon became my favorite person in Medjugorje—and remains so to this day. But I quickly noticed a wistfulness and regret at not being an integral part of the apparitions, even though she tried to hide it under an exterior of toughness. "One time is enough for me," she said. "I am blessed to see her and that is enough." Then with a dismissive wave she added, "I no want to have people coming to me all the time like Marija and other visionaries."

In September 1988, I arranged for Milka to come to the United States and stay with our family for three months. The visit had come about when I had felt that now-familiar inner urge from Our Lady, asking me to bring Milka to the States to learn fluent English so that she might function as a guide or assume a similar post.

This was a wonderful gift for my family and for Milka. She quickly learned enough English to speak about the apparitions at Medjugorje without a translator, and she did so on several occasions when I took her with me for scheduled talks. Word had spread that she was staying with us, and the invitations poured in.

However, it was during a short trip to speak in Charleston, South Carolina, less than a two-hour drive from our home in Myrtle Beach, that I finally discovered the full extent of Milka's personal pain of not having become a regular visionary at Medjugorje. It had been a wonderful trip. Milka had spoken to the audience in English without a hitch, when the appointed translator was unable to attend. She did so with ease and grace, and this had filled her with contentment.

On the trip home, she opened up. Relaxed and at ease, she calmly but strongly vented her frustrations, mainly at her mother for not letting her go back to the site of the first apparition the next day. And while she was happy for Marija, she was still haunted as to why she was not chosen to continue to see Our Lady, as though there was something wrong with her.

On returning to Medjugorje after three months of learning and traveling in the States, Milka continued to suffer from not being able to forget the memories of that first day of apparitions. What would have happened to her had she become a visionary? She just could not let go of her frustrations.

Having had a taste of the good life in the United States, Milka began a steady habit of staying out late and partying as much as possible. After a few months, she left her mother's home and went to Italy to be with her crowd of friends. She seemed determined to squeeze as much out of life as possible. This would eventually lead to other issues.

❧

It would take the love and determination of her big sister to bring Milka to grips with her problems. Now married and living in Monza, Italy, with her husband, Paolo, the Medjugorje visionary Marija was concerned with the character and reputation of the crowd her sister was hanging out with. She had always been the only one Milka would listen to, and often, it took a determined tough-love approach to reach her.

Finally, Marija had had enough. Milka had left her mother and was heading for a life of destruction. It was time to act if she was going to be able to save her little sister from a lifetime of problems. She and Paolo found Milka and took her to their home, where for the next several days, the two sisters talked and argued and talked some more.

Eventually, Marija and Paolo drove Milka back to Medjugorje to the home of their mother, who was no longer able to do the daily chores and take care of herself. For Milka this would become a special penance, as the resentment against her mother was still present.

But in time, the resentment passed, and a deep affection settled in its place. Taking care of her mother was a healing. Soon Milka met a young man named Jure from the nearby village of Ljbushski. They were engaged, and, within the year, married.

Milka is now the mother of three children. She travels twelve miles to Medjugorje almost daily to care for her mother, who is almost completely incapacitated. She does so with total dedication and love.

On a recent trip we met as we usually do when I am in Medjugorje. I dared to ask the question: Do you still resent not being a Medjugorje visionary?

Milka smiled that familiar smile I first saw in the little café where we met. "No, no. I am happy to be a wife and mother."

This time, I knew she meant it.

The question remains: Why are some people chosen for such a charismatic gift of being a visionary to apparitions of the Blessed Virgin Mary, while others, who possibly are more qualified by our human standards, are not? How does one receive the gift, as Milka did, and then lose it seemingly due to human error, in this case that of her mother's refusal to believe her?

There really is no humanly satisfying answer to this question. It is simply God's will.

However, usually over a period of time, there is indication by way of the fruits as to why a person is chosen for such a gift. Milka's sister Marija has proven in the past twenty-four years that she is truly a child of God, quite capable through humility, acceptance, capability, and action to do what is asked by Our Lady to convey her messages from heaven. She does so by thought, word, and deed. The same is true of the other Medjugorje visionaries.

Would Milka have done as well as one of the Medjugorje visionaries over the same period of time as her sister? We will never know. What is known is that Milka did eventually surrender to the will of God and become a wife and mother—and a true child of God.

Paradoxically, many people who *are* chosen to receive a spiritual gift, such as that of being a visionary or a locutionist or a spiritually gifted person of God, ask the question: Why me? This is a question that I often ask concerning the mission I was asked to do.

It took a while for me personally to find the answer. I believe it is the generic answer to all who ask the question. I found it in the "Joyful Mysteries" of the Holy Rosary, in the second mystery, which is now my favorite.

In this second joyful mystery, a teenage Mary travels a great distance to her older cousin Elizabeth's home, as requested by the Holy Spirit. As she enters the tiny courtyard, Elizabeth, upon seeing her, is filled with the Holy Spirit and says, "Who am I that the mother of my Lord should come to me?"

The answer I finally discovered is simple and direct: I am a child of God.

For the people involved in all of the stories contained here, the answer is the same. It just takes some longer to discover it, or to accept it, and then to do the best that can be done with what has been given.

May every child of God discover this awesome gift, as those involved in the stories contained here have done, and allow the child within to lead them to fulfillment of God's plan.

"Dear children! Also today I call you to prayer. Little children, believe that by simple prayer, miracles can be worked. Through your prayer you open your heart to God and He works miracles in your life. By looking at the fruits, your heart fills with joy and gratitude to God for everything He does in your life and, through you, also to others. Pray and believe little children, God gives you graces and you do not see them. Pray and you will see them. May your day be filled with prayer and thanksgiving for everything that God gives you. Thank you for having responded to my call."

Monthly message given to the visionary Marija, October 25, 2002.

EPILOGUE

As of this writing, the *Child* continues to lead His children through the apparitions of the Blessed Virgin Mary at Medjugorje. The Child has allowed His mother to appear daily now for twenty-four years and counting. When it will all end, no one knows, with the possible exception of the visionaries, and they have been instructed by the Blessed Virgin not to discuss it. In the meantime, she continues through her messages to lead her "dear children" to her Son.

And the children have responded. Over the twenty-four plus years, approximately thirty *million* people have made pilgrimage to Medjugorje. Tens of thousands of them have been young people. In comparison to past apparitions, such as Lourdes and Fatima, Medjugorje is arguably the highest in scope, popularity, and effect. It is especially so for young people.

Regardless of its history as a place of conversion for young and old, the human element still prevails. The majority of questions asked about Medjugorje are about the ten secrets the Virgin has given to the visionaries, especially since some of them are about catastrophic events that will affect the entire world. As might be expected, young people are the most curious.

In the early days of the apparitions, The Blessed Virgin told the visionaries that she would reveal to each of them ten future events—or secrets, as they were quickly labeled—that would occur after the apparitions were over. She stated that she would reveal them over a period of time, which continues. Once each visionary receives the tenth secret, the Virgin will no longer appear to them in daily apparition but will appear to them at least once annually. And once all of the visionaries have received all ten secrets, then the apparitions will cease and the secrets will begin to occur in sequence after a short period of time.

Three of the original six visionaries still see the Blessed Virgin Mary daily. The other three see her at least once a year, as she promised when their daily apparitions ended. Marija, Vicka, and Ivan continue to have the apparitions, and each has been given nine of the ten secrets promised. Mirjana, Ivanka, and Jakov now see the Blessed Virgin once a year. However, Mirjana now has apparitions on the second day of each month. This unprecedented event in the annuals of Marian history started several years ago and continues.

Despite the concern over the ten secrets, life in the village of Medjugorje is typical of past apparition sites. Commercialism is rampant; outsiders have moved in to take advantage of opportunity. Construction of new buildings and additions to homes to house even more pilgrims is constant. And bickering and debate as to the authenticity of the apparitions has not subsided.

The current bishop, Ratko Peric, denounces the apparitions as completely false at a far greater decibel level than did his predecessor, the late Pavo Zanic. Yet, the beloved Pope John Paul II, who died in April 2005, unofficially embraced the apparitions as authentic, urging bishops visiting Rome to go to Medjugorje, and stating that he wished to go himself. According to the visionary Ivan, he finally got his wish. Moreover, it served a far greater purpose.

Ivan stated that on the evening of the Pope's death, he was giving his testimony in a church in Massachusetts and had his daily apparition in front of a large audience. When the apparition was over, Ivan revealed to close friends and associates that something wonderful had happened.

The Blessed Virgin had appeared, alone, as usual at the appointed time. Suddenly, a young, radiant John Paul appeared at her left side. He was dressed in a white robe and was draped in a gold cape. "*This is my son,*" she told Ivan. "*He is with me.*"

The purpose of allowing Ivan—and all of us transformed by this spiritual miracle of the first magnitude—a special grace of seeing the earthly departed Pope John Paul II in heaven with his beloved Blessed Virgin Mary, is crystal clear: The reward for all who allow the *Child* to lead them is eternal life in heaven.

May the peace, grace, and love of Jesus be with each of you.

ACKNOWLEDGMENTS

No book publication is possible without great support from family, friends, and associates. I thank Paraclete Press, publishers of five of my books, for invaluable guidance, professionalism, and loyalty; and, especially Jon Sweeney for his outstanding editing and direction for this particular work. I thank those very special friends and supporters of the events of Medjugorje who have remained loyal and supportive throughout the years of involvement in the apparitions. They include Father Svetozar Kraljevic, Father Bill Elder, Father Ed Chalmers, Bob and Elaine Starbuck, Milanka Lachman, Jim and Sandi Culley, Arthur McClusky, Steve and Ana Shawl, Patricia Keane, Jim Gilboy, Paul Kellerman, Pat O'Mara, Jacqueline Butler, and Anne Helseby. Most especially, I thank the thousands of readers who keep the Medjugorje grace at maximum levels.

APPENDIX OF THE MONTHLY MESSAGES

Starting from June 2005, going back through January 2004

Message of June 25, 2005

"Dear children! Today I thank you for every sacrifice that you have offered for my intentions. I call you, little children, to be my apostles of peace and love in your families and in the world. Pray that the Holy Spirit may enlighten and lead you on the way of holiness. I am with you and bless you all with my motherly blessing. Thank you for having responded to my call."

Message of May 25, 2005

"Dear children, anew I call you to live my messages in humility. Especially witness them now when we are approaching the anniversary of my apparitions. Little children, be a sign to those who are far from God and His love. I am with you and bless you all with my motherly blessing. Thank you for having responded to my call."

Message of April 25, 2005

"Dear children, also today I call you to renew prayer in our families. By prayer and the reading of Sacred Scripture, may the Holy Spirit,

who will renew you, enter into your family. In this way, you become teachers of the faith in your family. By prayer and your love, the world will set out on a better way and love will begin to rule in the world. Thank you for having responded to my call."

Message of March 25, 2005

"Dear children, today I call you to love. Little children, love each other with God's love. At every moment, in joy and in sorrow, may love prevail and, in this way, love will begin to reign in your hearts. The risen Jesus will be with you and you will be His witnesses. I will rejoice with you and protect you with my motherly mantle. Especially, little children, I will watch your daily conversion with love. Thank you for having responded to my call."

Message of February 25, 2005

"Dear children, today I call you to be my extended hands in this world that puts God in the last place. You, little children, put God in the first place in your life. God will bless you and give you strength to bear witness to Him, the God of love and peace. I am with you and intercede for all of you. Little children, do not forget that I love you with a tender love. Thank you for having responded to my call."

Message of January 25, 2005

"Dear children, in this time of grace again I call you to prayer. Pray, little children, for unity of Christians, that all may be one heart. Unity will really be among you inasmuch as you will pray and forgive. Do not forget: Love will conquer only if you pray, and your heart will open. Thank you for having responded to my call."

Message of December 25, 2004

"Dear children! With great joy, also today I carry my Son Jesus in my arms to you; He blesses you and calls you to peace. Pray, little children, and be courageous witnesses of Good News in every situation. Only in this way will God bless you and give you everything you ask of Him in faith. I am with you as long as the Almighty permits me. I intercede for each of you with great love. Thank you for having responded to my call."

Message of November 25, 2004

"Dear children! At this time, I call you all to pray for my intentions. Especially, little children, pray for those who have not yet come to know the love of God and do not seek God the Savior. You, little children, be my extended hands and by your example draw them closer to my

heart and the heart of my Son. God will reward you with graces and every blessing. Thank you for having responded to my call."

Message of October 25, 2004

"Dear children! This is a time of grace for the family and, therefore, I call you to renew prayer. May Jesus be in the heart of your family. In prayer, learn to love everything that is holy. Imitate the lives of saints so that they may be an incentive and teachers on the way of holiness. May every family become a witness of love in this world without prayer and peace. Thank you for having responded to my call."

Message of September 25, 2004

"Dear children! Also today, I call you to be love where there is hatred and food where there is hunger. Open your hearts, little children, and let your hands be extended and generous so that, through you, every creature may thank God the Creator. Pray, little children, and open your heart to God's love, but you cannot if you do not pray. Therefore, pray, pray, pray. Thank you for having responded to my call."

Message of August 25, 2004

"Dear children! I call you all to conversion of heart. Decide, as in the first days of my coming here, for a complete change of your life. In this way, little children, you will have the strength to kneel and to open your hearts before God. God will hear your prayers and answer them. Before God, I intercede for each of you. Thank you for having responded to my call."

Message of July 25, 2004

"Dear children! I call you anew: Be open to my messages. I desire, little children, to draw you all closer to my Son Jesus; therefore, you pray and fast. Especially I call you to pray for my intentions, so that I can present you to my Son Jesus; for Him to transform and open your hearts to love. When you will have love in the heart, peace will rule in you. Thank you for having responded to my call."

Message of June 25, 2004

"Dear children! Also today, joy is in my heart. I desire to thank you for making my plan realizable. Each of you is important, therefore, little children, pray and rejoice with me for every heart that has converted and become an instrument of peace in the world. Prayer

groups are powerful, and through them I can see, little children, that the Holy Spirit is at work in the world. Thank you for having responded to my call."

Message of May 25, 2004

"Dear children! Also today, I urge you to consecrate yourselves to my heart and to the heart of my Son Jesus. Only in this way will you be mine more each day and you will inspire each other all the more to holiness. In this way joy will rule your hearts and you will be carriers of peace and love. Thank you for having responded to my call."

Message of April 25, 2004

"Dear children! Also today, I call you to live my messages even more strongly in humility and love so that the Holy Spirit may fill you with His grace and strength. Only in this way will you be witnesses of peace and forgiveness. Thank you for having responded to my call."

Message of March 25, 2004

"Dear children! Also today, I call you to open yourselves to prayer. Especially now, in this time of grace, open your hearts, little children,

and express your love to the Crucified. Only in this way, will you discover peace, and prayer will begin to flow from your heart into the world. Be an example, little children, and an incentive for the good. I am close to you and I love you all. Thank you for having responded to my call."

Annual Apparition To Mirjana, March 18, 2004:

The visionary Mirjana Dragicevic-Soldo had daily apparitions from June 24th, 1981, to December 25th, 1982. During the last daily apparition, Our Lady gave her the tenth secret and told her that she would appear to her once a year, on the 18th of March. It has been this way through the years.

This year Our Lady gave the following message:

"Dear children! Also today, watching you with a heart full of love, I desire to tell you that what you persistently seek, what you long for, my little children, is before you. It is sufficient that, in a cleaned heart, you place my Son in the first place, and then you will be able to see. Listen to me and permit me to lead you to this in a motherly way."

Message of February 25, 2004

"Dear children! Also today, as never up to now, I call you to open your hearts to my messages. Little children, be those who draw souls to God and not those who distance them. I am with you and love you all with a special love. This is a time of penance and conversion. From the bottom of my heart, I call you to be mine with all your heart and then you will see that your God is great, because He will give you an abundance of blessings and peace. Thank you for having responded to my call."

Message of January 25, 2004

"Dear children! Also today I call you to pray. Pray, little children, in a special way for all those who have not come to know God's love. Pray that their hearts may open and draw closer to my heart and the heart of my Son Jesus, so that we can transform them into people of peace and love. Thank you for having responded to my call."

ABOUT PARACLETE PRESS

Who We Are

Paraclete Press is an ecumenical publisher of books on Christian spirituality for people of all denominations and backgrounds.

We publish books that represent the wide spectrum of Christian belief and practice—Catholic, Orthodox, and Protestant.

We market our books primarily through booksellers; we are what is called a "trade" publisher, which means that we like it best when readers buy our books from booksellers, our partners in successfully reaching as wide an audience as possible.

We are uniquely positioned in the marketplace without connection to a large corporation or conglomerate and with informal relationships to many branches and denominations of faith, rather than a formal relationship to any single one. We focus on publishing a diversity of thoughts and perspectives—the fruit of our diversity as a company.

What We Are Doing

Paraclete Press is publishing books that show the diversity and depth of what it means to be Christian. We publish books that reflect the Christian experience across many cultures, time periods, and houses of worship.

We publish books about spiritual practice, history, ideas, customs, and rituals, and books that nourish the vibrant life of the church.

We have several different series of books within Paraclete Press, including the bestselling Living Library series of modernized classic texts, A Voice from the Monastery—giving voice to men and women monastics on what it means to live a spiritual life today, and Many Mansions—exploring the riches of the world's religious traditions and discovering how other faiths inform Christian thought and practice.